Postliberal Theology
and the Church
Catholic

Postliberal Theology and the Church Catholic

CONVERSATIONS WITH
George Lindbeck, David Burrell, and Stanley Hauerwas

Edited by John Wright

B
BakerAcademic
a division of Baker Publishing Group
Grand Rapids, Michigan

Published by Baker Academic
a division of Baker Publishing Group
P.O. Box 6287, Grand Rapids, MI 49516-6287
www.bakeracademic.com

Printed in the United States of America

Library of Congress Cataloging-in-Publication Data
Postliberal theology and the church catholic : conversations with George Lindbeck, David Burrell, and Stanley Hauerwas / edited by John W. Wright.
    p.   cm.
Includes bibliographical references and index.
ISBN 978-0-8010-3982-9 (pbk.)
    1. Postliberal theology. 2. Church—Unity. 3. Burrell, David B.—Interviews.
4. Hauerwas, Stanley, 1940– —Interviews. 5. Theologians—United States—Interviews. I. Lindbeck, George A. II. Burrell, David B. III. Hauerwas, Stanley 1940–
IV. Wright, John W.
BT83.595.L58 2012
230.092′273—dc23   2011039196

12   13   14   15   16   17   18   7   6   5   4   3   2   1

To
Reverend Katherine S. Wright
Chair of the Multi-Congregational Board,
The Church of the Nazarene in Mid-City, San Diego

Contents

Acknowledgments

In the late winter of 1984, Robert Louis Wilken, the professor in my first Christianity and Judaism in Antiquity PhD seminar at the University of Notre Dame, pressed into my hand a newly published volume called *The Nature of Doctrine: Religion and Theology in a Postliberal Age*. I had never heard of the author, a Yale Divinity School professor named George Lindbeck. I finished the book that night. Perhaps this book began there.

In the summer of 1984 I ran into Stanley Hauerwas at the second-floor copier in the Hesburgh Library at the University of Notre Dame. The next day he was to leave South Bend to begin his teaching post at Duke Divinity School. He kindly greeted me and I thanked him for his work, told him that I mourned never being able to study under him in class, and wished him well from one "Wesleyan" to another. Perhaps this book began there.

In the spring of 1991 I shared lunch with David Burrell when I served as a visiting professor teaching general education students at the University of Notre Dame. In the middle of the lunch, David spoke about his relationship with George Lindbeck when Burrell was chair of the Department of Theology at Notre Dame. Perhaps this book began there.

To speak of the beginnings of a book is to recognize how indebted one's life is to the gift God gives to us in others.

Acknowledgments remind us that none of our work is really our own, particularly one like this book. First, I need to thank George Lindbeck, David Burrell, and Stanley Hauerwas for their graciousness as they gathered for a conversation in the winter of 2007 in Kansas City, Missouri. While I had known David and Stanley when sojourning at the University of Notre Dame, I had never formally been their student; I had never even spoken to Professor Lindbeck until I called him in his retirement to inquire about his interest in taking part in a conversation with David and Stanley. Yet all three agreed to come to engage in these conversations only upon my request. Ron Benefiel, then president of Nazarene Theological Seminary, offered to sponsor the conversation that took place under the Hugh C. Benner endowed lectureship in memory of Hugh C. Benner, the founding president of NTS. Ironically, a "Benner scholarship" had helped pay for my undergraduate education at Mount Vernon Nazarene College. It was an honor to have the late Dr. Benner's daughter, Janet Miller, his son, Dr. Richard Benner, and his daughter-in-law, Dr. Patricia Benner, in attendance for the conversations.

Dr. John Hawthorne, then provost at Point Loma Nazarene University, provided early encouragement for the project, and later, paid travel expenses out of the Provost's Fund at PLNU for my participation in it. Monsignor Lorenzo Albacete of Communion and Liberation discussed the project with me in its early stages and enthusiastically embraced it. Monsignor Albacete was to interview Drs. Lindbeck, Hauerwas, and Burrell. Unfortunately he became ill immediately before the event and was unable to attend. I was required to stand in for him. Dr. Andy Johnson, professor of New Testament at Nazarene Theological Seminary, did the unrecognized work, for which I am thankful, in overseeing the local logistics for the entire event.

It has taken me too long to turn these interviews into this book. Perhaps it never would have been completed without a sabbatical granted by my institution, Point Loma Nazarene University. Jason Byassee, who attended the conversation, provided early encouragement to record the conversations in book form. Rodney Clapp guided the work through the contractual and editorial processes at Baker Academic and provided wise editorial suggestions. Professor Hauerwas read drafts of the chapters and provided encouragement and feedback. Dr. Mark Mann, director of the Wesleyan Center at Point Loma Nazarene University, provided keen eyes for reading portions of early drafts of the book, as did my young friend Professor Jonathan Tran of Baylor University. He is a much better judge of my writing than of NBA players. My wife, Rev. Kathy Wright, provided help in transcribing the oral conversations from NTS into typed prose, as did my daughter, Natasha Wright. To share in this project with them and my sons, Johnny, Carl, and Tony, has been a deep joy.

The book is dedicated to my wife of over thirty-one years, Rev. Kathy Wright. She has unswervingly supported me in this book as throughout all life. When she proclaims the Word of God in her preaching at the Church of the Nazarene in Mid-City, California, she helps me see why such a project is important. When she oversees pastors working harmoniously together in one building for seven different congregations from various regions throughout the world in a strange place called "San Diego," she helps make this work intelligible. For her witness and her help in this project, all I can do is give God thanks.

John W. Wright
Trinity Sunday, 2011

1

Introduction

Back to the Future

If modern philosophy can be seen as "post-medieval," then "post-modern" philosophy will have to be read as "post (post-medieval)."

—David Burrell[1]

It is hard enough to understand the past, let alone predict the future. Who in the middle of the 1980s predicted the dissolution of the Soviet Union in 1989? Looking back on the series of economic bubbles in the past twenty years, we now wonder why mainstream economists did not see the housing bubble that formed in the early 2000s. This inability to see what seems evident in retrospect has led to economic chaos throughout the world. It seems safe to say that unexpected, utterly contingent

1. David Burrell, "Religion and the University," *Crosscurrents* 56, no. 2 (Summer 2006), 157, available at http://www.crosscurrents.org/burrellsummer2006.pdf.

events characterize history more than the smooth, gradual statistical slopes of progress and decline.[2] History, like life, is full
of surprises.

Interpreted from within the history of a visible church catholic, the twentieth century proved both horribly grievous and
delightfully surprising. The sufferings of the first half of the
century paved the way for healing a thousand years of increased
fragmentation in the ecclesial body of Christ. Yet the later part
of the century witnessed new fissures in the church, even as God
changed its social location from its medieval European centers
to the Southern hemisphere and Asia.

It seems almost bizarre today to raise the question of the
visible unity of the church. Rifts within the church throughout
history appear too deep, and the truthfulness of theological
claims seems unintelligible when analyzed solely in light of
the immanent working of power in history. The question
of the visible unity of the church in faith and order seems
at best nostalgic, and at worst reactionary and oppressive.
Theological discourse in the West has tended to emphasize
vague humanistic ethical goods like "freedom" or "justice";
it has also sought to develop a marketable "group-identity"
for self-identification, meaning, and proselytism. "Denominations" seem natural, so natural that even those within
the Roman Catholic Church can call themselves part of a
"denomination."

In 1984 a theologian little known outside of ecumenical circles, George Lindbeck, published a small volume named *The
Nature of Doctrine*. Lindbeck's book sought to bridge earlier
Christian divisions, but did so in an inverse direction from the
general movement of Western culture, the Western academy,
and the church, particularly in the United States. The volume
quickly attracted attention far beyond what the author had

2. See, for instance, Nissim Nicholas Taleb, *The Black Swan: The Impact of the
Highly Improbable* (New York: Random House, 2007); Thomas Kuhn, *The Structures
of Scientific Revolutions* (Chicago: University of Chicago Press, 1962); and various
works by Michel Foucault, for instance, *Discipline and Punish: The Birth of the Prison*
(New York: Random House, 1975).

anticipated. It became a lightning rod both for what it advocated—a "postliberal approach" to Christian doctrine—and for what it criticized—"propositional-cognitive" and especially "experiential-expressivist" theological methods. Lindbeck's volume inadvertently touched a raw nerve that ran through theological and ecclesial circles.[3] As Lindbeck himself has commented, "The book seems to the left as a direct assault and by the right as a Trojan horse."[4]

In the 1980s theological scholarship was preoccupied with issues of method. Scholars quickly linked Lindbeck's work with that of his colleague at Yale, Hans Frei, and created a so-called Yale School. This new "school" of theology supposedly provided a new theological method based on a general theory of religion—a communally enclosed, intratextual, mediating theology. Interpreters separated Lindbeck's book from the pre-1960s theological movements that Lindbeck and his colleagues sought to advance, movements related to the ecumenical program found in the Lima Document of the World Council of Churches and its Catholic version in Vatican II.

The term *postliberal theology* still generates heat. Over twenty-five years after Lindbeck's publication, some continue to promote "postliberal theology" while others have declared and celebrated its demise.[5] Perhaps we should have expected the irony that a book on ecumenism would heighten fundamental divisions within Christian theological discourse. Lindbeck recognized that new sunderings had occurred in the Western

3. For a thorough review of the controversy in relation to Lindbeck's work, see Paul J. DeHart, *The Trial of the Witnesses: The Rise and Decline of Postliberal Theology* (Oxford: Blackwell, 2006), 32–41.

4. George Lindbeck, "Foreword to the German Edition of *The Nature of Doctrine*," in *The Church in a Postliberal Age*, ed. James Buckley (Grand Rapids: Eerdmans, 2003), 196.

5. Even though Paul J. DeHart spoke in 2006 of "the dismantling of postliberalism" (*Trial of the Witnesses*, 276), within the next year two books appeared that consciously identified themselves as "postliberal," one from a Protestant theologian (William Placher, *The Triune God: An Essay in Postliberal Theology* [Louisville: Westminster John Knox, 2007]) and one from a Roman Catholic theologian (Robert Barron, *The Priority of Christ: Toward a Postliberal Catholicism* [Grand Rapids: Brazos, 2007]).

church in the past two centuries that both simplified and com-
plicated its previous divisions (especially from the sixteenth
century onward).

This book seeks to place postliberal theology within the
broader stream of the "Tradition of the Great Church."[6] Postliberal theology, as we have known it, is radically liberal—a
movement of updating the faith given to the saints—at the same
time that it is radically conservative—nothing less than a return to the normative historical sources of the faith. It seeks to
faithfully carry on the life of the church catholic, especially as
seen in the lives of the saints—including those saints that many
would call "Protestant." While both Protestant and Catholic,
postliberal theology is neither Protestant nor Catholic in the way
these distinctions have been defined in the past several centuries.
Its greatest achievement has passed with barely a yawn—the
World Lutheran Confederation and the Catholic Church's Joint
Declaration on the Doctrine of Justification (1999).

6. In his introduction in *Scripture, Creed, Theology: Lectures on the History of
Christian Doctrine in the First Centuries*, ed. George A. Lindbeck (Eugene, OR:
Cascade, 2010), Lindbeck speaks of the "Great Church" as

> a relatively unified mainstream gradually coalescing in the course of the second
> century out of an initial multiplicity of often-competing groups claiming to
> be not only Christian but also, in the most significant cases, apostolic and
> catholic. . . . It grew in the course of the third century to embrace the vast
> majority of Christians. Naturally it defined orthodoxy for subsequent genera-
> tions. It viewed its understanding of the faith as in continuity with that of
> the apostles and treated those who disagreed (that is, heretics) as innovators
> who had distorted the faith once for all delivered to the saints. These seeming
> innovators, however, can sometimes be plausibly represented as survivors or
> conservers, marginalized heirs of versions of Christianity no less ancient than
> those to which the majority appealed. If they can be so understood, then
> doctrinal development is a matter of constructing orthodoxy rather than
> of developing (as Catholics since Newman have held) or distorting (as such
> liberal Protestants as von Harnack have maintained) the original deposit or
> experience of faith. (lxii–lxiii)

Significantly, Lindbeck continues, "the communities that developed in the 'orthodox' Great Church had no political, cultural, social or economic advantages; indeed,
they seem to have been the most persecuted of the professedly Christian groups.
Their victory can be plausibly—perhaps most plausibly—explained as a function of
their success in constructing unity-and-community-constituting polities, canonical
scriptures, liturgies, and rules of faith" (lxiii).

This theological program grew out of and developed its ecumenical potential as a response to a divided church whose witness was helpless—a church that had even supported the devastation that World War II wrought upon the world. For the postliberals Christian language is not merely verbal, but is encoded within the embodied life and practices of the ecclesial body and its individual members. The Christian witness to peace is inextricably bound to the ability of the church to live, speak, and confess in harmony. Postliberal theology addresses concerns for the unity of the church within a world devastated by violence and war.[7]

Postliberal theology, however, is not a nostalgic apologetics withdrawn from the philosophical and intellectual currents of the last half of the twentieth century. The first-generation

7. Robert Cathey, *God in Postliberal Perspective: Between Realism and Non-Realism* (Burlington, VT: Ashgate, 2009), has helpfully described postliberalism as "a set of shared convictions rooted in historic and contemporary Christian communities and some common tendencies in method (philosophic and theological)." He describes in depth the "family resemblance" of the three postliberals that he engages, David Burrell, William Placher, and Bruce Marshall:

> All are Trinitarians, yet with different emphases on the unity of God and Trinity of Persons. . . . They all distance themselves, explicitly or implicitly, from the strong revisions in the doctrine of God proposed by process theism. . . . All share a concern for how Christian testimony to God as Trinity engages religious pluralism, especially in relation to Jewish and Islamic testimony and reflection. All bring Scripture and Christian reflection into conversation with philosophy. But they seek to transform philosophical water into the wine of theology. . . . They share a common concern for the particularity of Christian convictions, language, and witness to God's reality in the world, but apply those convictions to all of reality, not merely the subjectivity of believers or the inter-subjectivity of the Christian community. From a contextual basis (Christian community, Scripture, and tradition), they make universal claims . . . yet do not appeal to foundations of certainty to justify those claims. Their approaches to the justification of contextual beliefs differ, but they all ascribe a role to the Holy Spirit in turning sinful creatures by various ways toward the truth, who is Jesus Christ. Their dialogue partners are both past (Aquinas, Barth) and present (any reader with some background in philosophy, world religions, or theology; fellow Christians and some Jewish and Islamic scholars share their interests). If theology is an ellipsis with two foci, one called "tradition" and the other called "the present context," their privileged focus is tradition (Scripture, creeds, liturgy, past theological masters), but their thought keeps moving around the ellipsis bringing both foci into dialogue. (123–24)

postliberal theologians discussed and interviewed in this volume have not withdrawn into their own fideistic, churchy intellectual ghetto. Though deeply rooted in the tradition of the Great Church, postliberal theologians have produced an old/new theological discourse through special attention to language. The postliberals have drunk deeply from the well of twentieth-century Anglo-American analytic philosophy, particularly as it intersects with the thought of Thomas Aquinas. Although the analytic philosophical tradition has dominated mainstream Anglo-American *philosophical* discourse, theologians—largely shaped by engagement with continental philosophy—have tended to neglect its theological helpfulness and have thus overlooked the analytic, Thomistic background for postliberal theology.

The purpose of this book is to reestablish postliberal theology's concern for the visible unity of the church catholic. The book centers on biographical interviews with George Lindbeck, David Burrell, and Stanley Hauerwas and a conversation between them on the present/future unity of the church.

As mentioned above, Lindbeck is the Yale Divinity School professor who coined the term *postliberal theology*. He has worked tirelessly for the visible unity of the church through his own writings and in ecumenical dialogues and working groups.

Professor Stanley Hauerwas is Gilbert T. Rowe Professor of Theological Ethics at Duke Divinity School; he is often linked with the postliberal program, and not without reason given the continual positive references to *The Nature of Doctrine* throughout his books. Hauerwas received cultural recognition (unusual for a contemporary theologian) when he was named "Best Theologian in America" in 2002 by *Time* magazine.

Our final theologian, David Burrell, does not regularly appear in the discussions of "postliberal" theologians.[8] An expert in the work of Thomas Aquinas, particularly as an exemplar of

---

8. An exception is the insightful work by Robert Cathey, *God in Postliberal Perspective*, particularly 124–37. The following interviews confirm Cathey's hypothesis about "Lindbeck's dependence on Burrell's interpretation" of Thomas and his doctrine of analogy (62n28).

Christian dialogue with Jews and Muslims, Burrell has worked at the boundaries of philosophy, historical philosophy and theology, interreligious dialogue, and contemporary theology. Burrell's significance within contemporary theology is generally underestimated. His friendships with both Lindbeck and Hauerwas, however, highlight the vitality of the analytic philosophical transformation of Thomistic thought in which all three theologians participate. He has coauthored essays for thirty years with Hauerwas, and his book *Aquinas: God and Action* was long used by Lindbeck in regular doctoral seminars on Thomas Aquinas at Yale.[9] The interviews stress the intersection of Burrell's life and thought with that of Lindbeck and Hauerwas, two recognized "postliberal" theologians. Renewed interest in Thomistic theology in recent decades has made their shared theological tradition more evident. As Burrell has stated, if the modern was fundamentally post-medieval, then the postmodern is the post (post-medieval). In the return, we learn to go forward.

From the perspective of this particular retrieval of Thomistic thought, the name *postliberal* as a theological school or method is a misnomer. Late nineteenth- and early twentieth-century Roman Catholic history and theology had formed itself as a bastion against liberal thought and politics. A neo-Thomist perspective dominated pre–Vatican II Catholicism, strongly distinguishing between nature and grace, philosophy and theology. Neo-Thomism held that grace built upon the foundation of nature like a parfait; philosophy provided a universal rationality upon which the church could then add specific claims based on revelation. Such a Catholicism would interpret postliberalism as a hopeless capitulation to the modernist tradition—as have some, not accidently, within conservative Protestant circles.

9. In the foreword to the second edition, Burrell notes, "This exploration of Thomas Aquinas's philosophical theology, decidedly 'unorthodox' at the time of its original publication, had the good fortune to be employed extensively, notably at Yale and Cambridge, by my eminent colleagues George Lindbeck and Nicholas Lash" (David B. Burrell, *Aquinas: God and Action*, 2nd ed. [Scranton, PA: University of Scranton Press, 2008]).

Lindbeck's, Burrell's, and Hauerwas's works are postliberal
only from the perspective of late twentieth-century European
and American thought and ecclesial life.

Of course, if postliberalism is a misnomer, then the term
"Yale School" has even less utility.[10] While all three persons'
lives intersected with Yale University, they had little direct relationship with each other at the time. A depth of friendship
and interaction characterized the relationship of George Lindbeck to another member of the "Yale School," Hans Frei, but
their theological programs and backgrounds differed radically.
Lindbeck writes as an ecumenist from his training in medieval
Catholic thought, particularly under the impact of Thomas
Aquinas; Frei writes as a historian of modern Christian thought,
particularly under the impact of Karl Barth.

The title *postliberalism* itself grants too much to the obsession
with methodological schools that arose in the 1970s as a result
of cultural, intellectual, and institutional shifts (which these
three thinkers have resisted). It reduces their theological thought
to a contemporary option available for individual choice if so
suited—an item on the menu of expressive entrées for scholarly
or pastoral consumption. Perhaps it is more accurate to speak
of "postliberalism" as a contemporary retrieval of Augustinian
Thomism through interaction with twentieth-century linguistic
philosophy.[11]

The theologians discussed in this book provide a trajectory
for theological thought and ecclesial life from the center of the
Western Christian theological tradition. These thinkers also
adopted certain movements within twentieth-century analytic
philosophy as tools to help promote the visible unity of the
church. In words that characterized the renewal of the Catholic

10. DeHart helpfully notes this point in his discussions of the distinctions between
the theological programs of Hans Frei and George Lindbeck. See *Trial of the Witnesses*, esp. 242–45.

11. For the propriety of this convergence, see the wonderful essay by Joseph Incandela, "Similarities and Synergy: An Augustinian Reading of Aquinas and Wittgenstein," in *Grammar and Grace: Reformulations of Aquinas and Wittgenstein*, ed.
Jeffrey Stout and Robert MacSwain (London: SCM, 2004), 20–54.

Church at Vatican II, the theologians have lived and written as a means of *aggiornamento* (the updating of the language of the faith) through *ressourcement* (a return to the vital sources of the Christian tradition in Scripture and the Great Church). They have done so in order to work toward a visibly united church in our sojourn through the late modernity of the late twentieth and early twenty-first centuries.

The historical depth, intellectual vitality, contemporary relevance, and theological and philosophical truthfulness of Professors Lindbeck, Burrell, and Hauerwas only partially explain the attention and controversy that have attended the reception of their texts. Their analytic Augustinian Thomism provides a faithful expression of the Christian tradition and is an excellent intellectual resource for responding to the increased pluralism and secularism of North America and Europe. By granting insight into the histories of three central postliberal theologians, this book endeavors to help others within the church, novice and learned, to access this tradition as a means to witness creatively amid the "time between the times" in which we live. To understand both the power of their witness and the controversies they have spawned, we have to understand how they maintained a theological agenda that was deeply undercut by various cultural and institutional shifts in Western society in the 1960s. It is to this wider intellectual, cultural, and institutional background that we will turn as a context for the individual stories and observations that follow.

2

The Silent Shifting
of Tectonic Plates

"Let us imagine that the tectonic plates of our culture are shifting
in such a way as to encourage Christians once again to return
to their ecumenical roots."

George Lindbeck[1]

It is perhaps hard for North Americans to understand the theological trauma suffered in the church in Europe in the first half
of the twentieth century. North American theologians have
reflected extensively on Christian theological complicity in the
atrocity of the Shoah. However, the violence of Christians killing Christians in World Wars I and II has not occasioned pro-
longed reflection, perhaps because of a deeply held conviction

1. George Lindbeck, "The University and Ecumenism," in *Justification and the
Future of the Ecumenical Movement*, ed. William G. Rusch (Collegeville, MN: Liturgical Press, 2003), 10.

of American exceptionalism that justified the violence of the Allied cause. The military devastation of Europe, North Africa, and western and eastern Asia, however, made the tragedy of the fragmented church obvious for all to see. Perhaps it is not accidental that 1949 found both John Howard Yoder (a leading voice of Christian pacifism) and George Lindbeck in a France devastated by the Vichy regime's cooperation with Nazi Germany. Perhaps it should not surprise us that both became deeply involved in the ecumenical endeavors of the World Council of Churches, and both deeply interfaced with Roman Catholicism. Ecumenicity engaged the finest theological minds of the era, particularly in Europe. The movement toward the visible unity of the church catholic culminated in the Lima Statement of the World Council of Churches in 1961. By this time, Roman Catholicism had also undergone a remarkable inner transformation in order to address the scandal of a divided church whose own life contradicted its witness to the world of the possibilities of reconciliation and peace.[2]

The lives and theological programs of George Lindbeck, David Burrell, and Stanley Hauerwas come into clearer focus when we understand them in light of the deep cultural, intellectual, and institutional shifts that occurred in Western culture in the 1960s. The three scholars had diverse personal and ecclesial backgrounds; however, pre-1960s philosophical, ecclesial, and theological trends enabled the growth of their common friendship and overlapping interests in the decades that followed. These trends culminated at Vatican II, the twenty-first Ecumenical Council of the Roman Catholic Church. Pope John XXIII called the council in 1959, and Catholic bishops and invited observers attended it in Rome from 1962 through 1965. Vatican II makes clear the threads that hold together the lives and writings of Lindbeck, Burrell, and Hauerwas. Through their work, one discovers how the renewal of the church prayed for

2. See the excellent narrative of how the ecumenical task became central to the mission of the Roman Catholic curia provided by Jerome B. Vereb, *Because He Was German: Cardinal Bea and the Origins of Roman Catholic Engagement in the Ecumenical Movement* (Grand Rapids: Eerdmans, 2006).

by John XXIII in Vatican II moved silently beyond Roman Catholicism into other branches of the church catholic.

Perhaps this statement surprises us. The reception of Vatican II has been anything but smooth and uncontroversial. From the time of John XXIII's calling of Vatican II to Paul VI's closing of the council, profound, tectonic shifts had occurred in Western culture. These shifts reframed the very institutional context in which theological discourse occurred, particularly in North America. Lindbeck, Burrell, and Hauerwas all have refused to see the new "Age of Authenticity" as normative.[3] They instead have continued to develop pre-1960s philosophical and ecclesial trajectories as a means of engaging the contemporary world and renewing the witness of the church catholic. In the process they have swum upstream in the institutional matrix of North American culture. The resistance has not stopped them from continuing their programs, though; they have met their context with a critical intellectual acumen that has made their work difficult to ignore. Yet the institutional and cultural complexity that they have faced has made their work often subject to misunderstanding, much like Vatican II itself. They do not quite fit within the categories that seem natural to post-1960s North American culture, but therein lies the promise of their stories and their work for the future.

Mid-Twentieth Century Theological Renewal in Roman Catholicism: *Ressourcement*, Catholic Ecumenism, and Nature and the Supernatural in the *Nouvelle Théologie*

To begin our discussion of the first-generation postliberals with pre–Vatican II Roman Catholic thought may seem bizarre. Only Burrell is Roman Catholic (though his life and thought are intelligible only in light of the post–Vatican II Roman Catholic Church); Lindbeck is Lutheran; and Hauerwas, Methodist-Episcopal. Their work, however, continues the insights found within a particular constellation of largely French Roman Catholic theologians who

3. See Charles Taylor, *A Secular Age* (Cambridge, MA: Belknap, 2007), 473–504.

began their careers before Vatican II and remained active within and after the council. This loose group of thinkers shared a family resemblance in their active, academic theological work for the church, which was called the "*nouvelle théologie*"[4] or the *ressourcement* (a return to the classical, historic sources of the life of the church) movement.[5] Lindbeck, Burrell, and Hauerwas did not, however, relegate these theologians to an isolated niche as historical "Roman Catholic theologians" who engaged inner-Roman Catholic struggles for Catholic identity. The first generation of postliberal thinkers incorporated the basic theological insights of this group into a program that has reached into mainline and evangelical Protestant networks and the North American theological academy and beyond.[6]

---

4. A. N. Williams, in "The Future of the Past: The Contemporary Significance of the *Nouvelle Théologie*," *International Journal of Systematic Theology* 7 (2005), aptly describes the *nouvelle théologie* not as a movement per se but as a "common sensibility and vision":

> If we are to speak of the nouvelle théologie, let alone designate it as a movement of some sort, we must do so with some delicacy, therefore, but these considerations do not in themselves invalidate using the term altogether, for the significance of this theology subsists, not solely in the value of the contributions of individuals, but in the broader trends observable across the work they collectively produced. If it is an exaggeration to speak of a movement in any formal sense, we may still speak of one in the sense of a common sensibility and vision, not a system so much as a spirit. (348)

Such a position concurs with the analysis of Jürgen Mettepenningen:

> The expression nouvelle théologie is a cluster concept: a banner representing a variety of visions. . . . [T]he core ambition of each of the thinkers discussed in these pages is ultimately the same: to restore contact between theology and the living faith and thus also with the sources of the faith. To this end, the new theologians rejected every theological system that revolved around the system itself rather than around the faith: a system that caused the sources to clot and congeal, that reduced theologians from days long past to an authority while ignoring the actual content of their works in the name of the system. (*Nouvelle Théologie—New Theology: Inheritor of Modernism, Precursor of Vatican II* [New York: T&T Clark, 2010], 141)

5. Brian Daley has argued that this sensibility was "really about the rediscovery of sacramental modes of thought, through renewed contact with Christian authors who thought and read scripture in sacramental as well as literal terms" (Daley, "The *Nouvelle Théologie* and the Patristic Revival: Sources, Symbols, and the Science of Theology," *International Journal of Systematic Theology* 7 [2005]: 382).

6. Even Protestant evangelical thought has recently taken up interest in and the agenda of the *nouvelle théologie/ressourcement* movement. See, most recently, Hans

Two particular *ressourcement* theologians, Yves Congar and Henri de Lubac, may help us understand the first-generation postliberals in the context of Vatican II.[7] Avery Cardinal Dulles said of Congar that "Vatican II could almost be called Congar's Council";[8] and David Schindler has pointed to the "near-identical affirmation of an organic relation between Christology and anthropology"[9] in Vatican II and de Lubac. Though Congar and de Lubac were controversial within Roman Catholicism before Vatican II, their impact is widely acknowledged to be present in the documents of Vatican II. Their influence, however, has been lost as a backdrop for the postliberal theological program.

Congar's *Divided Christendom*, published in French in 1938, pulled the Roman Catholic Church into twentieth-century ecumenism kicking and screaming—at him. Congar shifted and deepened the terms of the ecumenical discussion, arguing that it concerned the very catholicity of the church. He did so in profoundly Roman Catholic terms, so much so that as Fergus Kerr observes, "it is difficult to imagine why colleagues and authorities in Rome were so worried about Congar's principles of Catholic ecumenism."[10] As Douglas Koskela has argued, "Congar re-worked the notion of *vestigia Ecclesiae* to suggest that non-Catholic bodies maintained elements of the genuine church of Christ that allowed an imperfect though real communion with the visible Catholic Church."[11]

Boersma, *Nouvelle Théologie and Sacramental Ontology: A Return to Mystery* (Oxford: Oxford University Press, 2009). Baker Academic, InterVarsity, and Eerdmans have all developed book series arising out of evangelical interest in *ressourcement*. In mainline North American Protestant thought, one can see this interest in the "canonical theism" of William Abraham and his students. See William Abraham, Jason Vickers, and Natalie van Kirk, eds., *Canonical Theism: A Proposal for Theology and the Church* (Grand Rapids: Eerdmans, 2008).

7. Mettepenningen places Congar in a "first phase" of the *nouvelle théologie* and de Lubac in a "second phase"; see *Nouvelle Théologie*, 41–47, 77–79, and 95–114.

8. Avery Dulles quoted in Fergus Kerr, *Twentieth-Century Catholic Theologians: From Neoscholasticism to Nuptial Mysticism* (Oxford: Blackwell, 2007), 34.

9. David L. Schindler, introduction to Henri de Lubac, *The Mystery of the Supernatural* (New York: Herder and Herder, 1998), xxvii.

10. Kerr, *Twentieth-Century Catholic Theologians*, 40.

11. Douglas M. Koskela, *Ecclesiality and Ecumenism: Yves Congar and the Road to Unity* (Milwaukee: Marquette University Press, 2008), 12.

Congar denied an invisible, spiritual end for ecumenism. The movement to overcome the sinful fragmentation of the church must "make explicit, perfect and visible that secret and imperfect membership of the Church that is already theirs [Protestants' and Orthodox's]."[12] As a result Congar emphasized a dialectic movement between the outward, embodied, visible church on the one hand and its inward, spiritual experiences on the other. Congar did not deny the inward, experiential dynamic as important for ecumenical discussions; rather he saw the outward and external as prior to the internal ontologically (though perhaps not methodologically) for actual ecumenical discussions:

> From this point of view of integration in the visible unity of the Church, which must be our ultimate objective, all this is of primary importance. It is quite true that in the Church the outward imparts the inward; dogmas teach and increase faith, sacramental rites teach and augment the inward gift of grace, and so on. But it is also true that dogmas are an outcome and an expression of faith, and all institutions and forms of worship are an outcome and expression of the inward Christian life under the guidance of the Holy Ghost. To find the Church in its completeness we may proceed from the outward form to the inward life, which is the normal way of a Catholic, born within the institution and impelled by the grace of God to find in it the sources of spiritual life. But it is also possible to proceed from the inner realities to their outward and visible expression, and this is obviously the most likely way for world-wide reunion.[13]

For Congar, the outward and visible gives rise to the inward and experiential, but at the same time one may work backwards, for ecumenical purposes, to relate the "inner realities" to these outward and visible expressions.

The search to achieve the visible unity of the church led Congar to study the relationship between "tradition and traditions"

12. M. J. Congar, *Divided Christendom: A Catholic Study of the Problem of Reunion* (London: Centenary, 1939), 259.
13. Ibid., 266.

in the history of the church.[14] Reacting to a strict, ahistorical, propositional notion of doctrine, Congar argued that tradition "in its historical journey, is as much development as it is memory and conservation."[15] Tradition, even its doctrinal statements, is the church's passing on of realities already embedded within the concrete life of a particular people:

> Tradition . . . is the communication of the entire heritage of the apostles, effected in a different way from that of their writings. We must try to define it more precisely and describe the original way in which it was done. It was not by discursive means, with all the accurate and precise formulation that this allows; it was by means of the concrete experience of life and of the familiar everyday realities of existence. It could well be compared to all that is implied by the idea of upbringing as opposed to instruction.[16]

The concern for the visible unity of the church catholic led Congar to recognize that we cannot reduce the church's tradition—its doctrine, liturgy, life, and ethics—to universal, objective, abstract statements dispersed among various discrete areas of life. Tradition is thicker, more concrete, more embodied: "For tradition to exist—tradition understood as the environment in which we receive the Christian faith and are formed by it—it must be borne by those who, having received it, live by it, and pass it on to others, so that they may live by it in their turn. Tradition, like education, is a living communication whose content is inseparable from the act by which one living person hands it on to another."[17] The concern for the visible unity of the church sensitized Congar to the realization that the church

14. See Yves Congar, *Tradition and Traditions: An Historical and Theological Essay* (London: Burns & Oates, 1966). For a recent review of the work, see John Webster, "Purity and Plenitude: Evangelical Reflections on Congar's *Tradition and Traditions,*" *International Journal of Systematic Theology* 7 (2005): 399–424.

15. Yves Congar, *The Meaning of Tradition*, trans. A. N. Woodrow (1964; repr., San Francisco: Ignatius, 2004), 122.

16. Ibid., 22.

17. Ibid., 24.

itself was necessarily a concrete, historical, embodied organism visible in the world.[18]

The work of the young Congar paved the way for the early writings of Henri de Lubac. Yves Congar's series Unam Sanctam published Henri de Lubac's first major book, *Catholicism: Christ and the Common Destiny of Man*, in 1939. Another, later book, *The Mystery of the Supernatural*, translated into English in 1967, has impacted English-language theological scholarship more than de Lubac's other works. In this book, de Lubac makes his earlier research on the underlying logic of the relationship between grace and nature (or the supernatural and nature, or God and creation) in the Christian tradition more easily accessible to an English-language audience.

Within a pre–Vatican II Roman Catholic context that had dissociated the natural and supernatural "realms," de Lubac argues that humanity by nature has a supernatural end—a sense of a lack that indicates the desire for God. Some hear him developing categories similar to those in the Protestant liberal and Catholic modernist position. De Lubac, however, argues that isolating the supernatural from nature ultimately leads to collapsing the supernatural into nature, the very logic of Protestant liberal and Catholic modernist thought: "All the values of the supernatural order, all those which characterize the present relationship between man and God in our economy of grace, will be gradually reabsorbed into that 'purely natural' order that has been imagined (and I say 'imagined' advisedly)."[19] Within the categories of modernity, "nature" requires that the

18. Hans Boersma states,
   One of Congar's most significant accomplishments was his combination of a sacramental ecclesiology with a salvation-historical focus. Sacramental ontology and history were not mutually exclusive categories for Congar. He maintained that whenever an ecclesiology focused unduly on the Pasch of Christ and on the institution of the Church, the result was a weakening of the sacramental reality (*res*) of the Church; at the same time, a single-minded focus on the Parousia and a corresponding neglect of the visible reality of the Church undermined the historical and provisional character of the Church (*sacramentum*). (Boersma, *Nouvelle Théologie and Sacramental Ontology*, 280–81)
19. De Lubac, *Mystery of the Supernatural*, 39.

"supernatural" conform to nature's own givenness: "Everything that now comes to us by the grace of God is thus withdrawn from the 'supernatural' properly so called of our present economy, and 'naturalized.'"[20]

Revelation becomes collapsed into what nature has already given, and God is placed into the immanent flow of history. Though de Lubac doesn't explicitly name Protestant liberalism as his target, it seems apparent that he recognizes this logic of "naturalizing the supernatural"[21] as characteristic of the Protestant liberal tradition: "It seems to me that this line of thinking leads to a natural morality pure and simple, which must tend to be a morality without religion—or at least with only a natural religion 'which is itself only one natural moral virtue among others.'"[22] Karl Barth was not the only theologian in the mid-twentieth century who criticized the basic modernist presuppositions at the core of Protestant liberalism![23]

De Lubac argues that the historical logic of the church on the relationship between the supernatural and nature is exactly the inverse of "naturalizing the supernatural." Nature always finds its beginning, sustenance, and end in God. We do not move from

20. Ibid., 40.

21. The phrase is taken from John Milbank's *Theology and Social Theory: Beyond Secular Reason*, 2nd ed. (London: Blackwell, 2006), 224. Milbank himself depends upon de Lubac's work.

22. De Lubac, *Mystery of the Supernatural*, 47.

23. De Lubac writes,

> It is chiefly a question of a "historical" immanentism, concentrating completely upon history, and envisaging the end of its development as a "universal reconciliation" which, both in itself and in the means needed to achieve it, would exclude everything supernatural. Where it is sometimes deceptive is when this immanentism of our age easily develops a dialectic of transcendence actually within the human being. It becomes all the more attractive as, presenting itself as the heir of Christianity (at last fully understood), far from rejecting it, it claims at last to fulfill perfectly the hopes awakened by Christ in men's hearts; and it is all the more formidable in being borne along on the most powerful current of thought in the age, and in presenting itself as making the only valid response to the challenge of historicity. I realize that the only way to "refute" it is by absorption, and I am confident that Christian thinking, once again, will be adequate to the task. (Ibid., xxxvi)

nature in order to explain or grasp the supernatural. Nor are we left with an arational fideism of a theological realm relevant only to faith. Rather, "it is, on the contrary, nature which is explained in the eyes of faith by the supernatural, as required for it."[24] Reason and faith do not correspond to isolated realms of nature and revelation. As the supernatural grounds and exalts nature to its true end in the supernatural, faith ensures and empowers reason. Simultaneously reason empowers faith to operate reasonably so that, together, humans might find the natural end of their temporal life in the eternally Triune God. Nature is never "given"; it is always "gift."

Like Congar, de Lubac recognizes that this theological position emphasizes the concrete, empirical world in which we live, but a world that is not closed in upon itself—a nature that is never completely "natural." Creation is held open by nature to that which is radically beyond it, that is, to the God who exceeds the very categories of the human mind: "It is always within the real world, within a world whose supernatural finality is not hypothetical but a fact, and not by following any supposition that takes us out of the world, that we must seek an explanation of the gratuitousness of the supernatural—in so far as the human mind can do so."[25] According to de Lubac, Catholic Christian ontology claims that in creation nature is always already graced; humans manifest this grace with a natural desire for our end in God.

De Lubac emphasizes that this lack—the natural human desire for that which transcends the concrete human being—never determines the character of the divine gift. The created order may make no demands on God. Humans find their true end only in revelation, that is, Jesus Christ:

24. Ibid., 95.

25. Ibid., 62. While de Lubac's historical analysis sought to uncover the underlying logic or grammar of what Congar would call the "Tradition," he thought that this grammar itself required that theology always be concrete and embodied: "Theology is not, or ought not to be, a buildup of concepts by which the believer tries to make the divine mystery less mysterious, and in some cases to eliminate it altogether. To reject this idea of theology does not mean that we think of it as something less ambitious, but quite the reverse: it is by rejecting this idea that we lift it above human banality" (178).

In itself that desire remains none the less hidden "in the ontological depths," and only the Christian revelation makes it possible to interpret either its indications or its meaning correctly. It is revelation which brings a final judgment to bear on all this human evidence: it condemns its *hubris*, estimates its deviations and brings to light its core of truth. Desire to see God, desire to be united with God, desire to be God: we find all these, or similar phrases, outside Christianity and independent of it. But how equivocal they all are![26]

Grace enables the concrete, bodily life of a human being to find its end in the body of Jesus Christ in preparation for our final end eternally in God. The real "nature" of the world only becomes manifest to humans through faith in Jesus Christ. As David Schindler states, only in this way may we "secure theologically the truth of creation as understood in the Gospel, which requires a non-divine subject that is nonetheless always already, in the one order of history, invited to participate in the divine trinitarian *communion* revealed in Jesus Christ."[27] According to de Lubac, the historic Christian tradition taught that human beings find their true divine vocation in Jesus Christ: his life, teachings, death, and resurrection.

Congar and de Lubac practiced *ressourcement* to rediscover the "grammar" of the historic Christian tradition before the distortions of modernity. Through their historical research, they sought to address the concrete challenges of the church in the modern world, a world that they had seen destroyed by wars twice during their lives. Their work combined a particular constellation of themes—God and creation, Christology, the unity of the church—to help contribute to the concrete, visible life of the church for the sake of the world. The themes constituted what became the main concerns of the Second Vatican Council.

As the interviews in subsequent chapters will show, Lindbeck, Burrell, and Hauerwas directly and indirectly participated in the theological backdrop that the *nouvelle théologie* helped

26. Ibid., 222.
27. David Schindler, introduction to de Lubac, *Mystery of the Supernatural*, xxvi.

create. This backdrop came together dramatically in the Second Vatican Council. Unknown to anyone at the time, however, the very historical and cultural forces that produced this powerful vision had begun to undermine it by the time the council began disseminating its texts. Even as the *ressourcement* movement, including the work of Karl Barth, came to its fullest expression, it became a subterranean minority voice, particularly in the dominant Protestant academic theology in North America. Lindbeck, Burrell, and Hauerwas, the first generation of the postliberal theologians, implicitly produced and renewed this program decades after it had ceased to be fashionable.

Vatican II, the Culture of Authenticity, and Postliberalism

The ecumenical and the *ressourcement* interests of the *nouvelle théologie* dramatically came together in John XXIII's charge for the Second Vatican Council. In retrospect, one can see that the council faithfully executed the task given to it by John XXIII in his opening speech. The speech moved from the general to the specific: after addressing the nature of previous ecumenical councils, John XXIII emphasized the Second Vatican Council's task to promote "The Unity of the Christian and Human Family." The speech rose to a climax with an extensive quote from St. Cyprian:

> The Church, surrounded by divine light, spreads her rays over the entire earth. This light, however, is one and unique and shines everywhere without causing any separation in the unity of the body. She extends her branches over the whole world. By her fruitfulness she sends ever farther afield her rivulets. Nevertheless, the head is always one, the origin one for she is the one mother, abundantly fruitful. We are born of her, are nourished by her milk, we live of her spirit. (*De Catholicae Eccles. Unitate*, 5)

The pope concluded:

> Venerable brothers, such is the aim of the Second Vatican Ecumenical Council, which, while bringing together the Church's

best energies and striving to have men welcome more favorably the good tidings of salvation, prepares, as it were and consolidates the path toward that unity of mankind which is required as a necessary foundation, in order that the earthly city may be brought to the resemblance of that heavenly city where truth reigns, charity is the law, and whose extent is eternity. (Cf. St. Augustine, Epistle 138, 3)[28]

It was not merely the tensions of the Cold War that framed Vatican II. Vatican II arose from the tragedy of millions of deaths in war that the church—Protestant, Catholic, and Orthodox—condoned, or at least was not able to resist from the European epicenter of its medieval heritage.[29] Pastoral renewal was to serve the cause of Christian reunion, which was in turn to provide a witness to the unity of humanity, a unity that would make war obsolete. As Fergus Kerr states, John XXIII hoped "to reform the Church explicitly in order to bring about reunion among Christians."[30]

As with most things about the council, such an interpretation remains contested. Giuseppe Alberigo in *The History of Vatican II* separates John XXIII's speech from its context of working for the visible unity of the church; instead he reads the speech in terms of theological methodology per se. Alberigo reads Pope John's call to *aggiornamento*, the updating of the faith, as a means of translating doctrine into language that would influence persons formed by the modern institutions of the liberal or Marxist nation-states. He focuses his interpretation

28. John XXIII, "Opening Speech for Council of Vatican II," October 11, 1962, available at *Our Lady's Warriors*, http://www.ourladyswarriors.org/teach/v2open.htm.

29. As Jerome-Michael Vereb writes, "Through the struggles of the Nazi debut, the Second World War, and the Cold War, the idea of ecumenism took on a sense of practical urgency, which gave it impetus and brought it from seed to shoot" (*Because He Was German*, 57).

30. Kerr, *Twentieth-Century Catholic Theologians*, 37. Kerr repeats his interpretation later as well: "Everyone was amazed, and many dismayed, when the elderly, 'transitional' Pope John XXIII announced his decision, on 25 January 1959, to hold a Council, foreseeing an agenda which would renew the life of the Church, bringing its teaching, discipline and organization up to date (*aggiornamento*) in order explicitly to facilitate the reunion of all Christians" (ibid., 151).

on John XXIII's statement: "The substance of the ancient doctrine of the deposit of faith is one thing, and the way in which it is presented is another. And it is the latter that must be taken into great consideration with patience if necessary, everything being measured in the forms and proportions of a magisterium which is predominantly pastoral in character."[31] According to Alberigo, "This was an important methodological guideline, since it situated the work of the council fathers at the heart of the Christian message, while at the same time urging them to present this message to the world in an updated way."[32] In this interpretation, the methodological "spirit" of the council moved the Roman Catholic Church into the social, intellectual, and political categories of the modern world.

The "kernel-and-husk" analogy used by John XXIII opened the door to different interpretations of the council. It led particularly to the conflict on whether to interpret Vatican II according to its documents or its "spirit." In the short time from John XXIII's calling of the council to its final adjournment and promulgation, deep cultural and institutional shifts had occurred. The prominent philosopher Charles Taylor calls this shift a movement from "The Culture of Mobilization" to "The Culture of Authenticity."[33] This shift effectively ended the cultural dynamics that had moved the church toward a concern for its visible unity. Instead, concerns to translate the historic

---

31. John XXIII, "Opening Speech."

32. Giuseppe Alberigo, *History of Vatican II*, vol. 2, *The Formation of the Council's Identity: First Period and Intersession* (Maryknoll, NY: Orbis, 1998), 17. John W. O'Malley follows this methodological interpretation of John XXIII's speech:

> In its understated way the address was in fact remarkable. It said that the council should take a positive approach; it should look forward; it should not be afraid to make changes in the church wherever appropriate; it should not feel constrained to stay within the old methods and forms, as if hermetically sealed off from modern thought; it should look to human unity, which suggested an approach that emphasized commonalities rather than differences; it should encourage cooperation with others; it should see its task as pastoral. The speech also suggested, or could be understood to suggest, that the council take a large view of its task, not limiting its purview simply to members of the Catholic Church. (*What Happened at Vatican II* [Cambridge, MA: Belknap, 2008], 96)

33. See Charles Taylor, *A Secular Age* (Cambridge, MA: Belknap, 2007), 423–504.

faith into new, more "relevant" expressions for "modern" humans came to predominate. "Plurality of expressions" rather than "unity of faith" became the rallying cry of theologians and churches alike—the celebration of diversity over visible harmony.

In Henri de Lubac's terms, the cultural task became to naturalize the supernatural. Theologians, having lost the institutionally imposed, hermetically sealed "transcendental realm of revelation" as a counterweight to the immanent frame of history and nature in neo-Thomism, began to think of God in light of the immanence of nature and history. The *nouvelle théologie*'s argument that we must understand nature and history in light of the mystery of God came to be seen as a conservative, authoritarian reaction to impulses for theological expressions of human authenticity within history. The impulse to find the beginning and end of all things in God had empowered the postwar quest for the visible unity of the church; the church, as all things, is raised up and perfected in its harmonious end in the Triune God. From the perspective of the *nouvelle théologie*, an invisible unity of the church that was manifested in an expressive pluralism of human experiences contradicted their deepest convictions.

We can easily underestimate how deeply a concern for a visible unity of the church dominated Christian theological discourse following the "Great Wars" of the twentieth century. We are now quick to remember that Swiss Reformed theologian Karl Barth called the doctrine of the analogy of being (which he attributed to Roman Catholicism) "the invention of the antichrist" in the preface to volume 1 of *Church Dogmatics*; but we fail to remember that he completed the sentence: "because of it it is impossible ever to become a Roman Catholic, *all other reasons for not doing so being to my mind short-sighted and trivial*."[34]

---

34. Karl Barth, *Church Dogmatics* I/1 (1928; London: T&T Clark, 2004), xiii (emphasis added). One wonders about the implications of this quote for reading Barth if, as recent research has suggested, he was mistaken in his reading of Roman Catholic thought precisely at this point.

This loss of awareness of the church catholic as the setting for theological discourse happened in the tumultuous decade of the 1960s. The social turmoil manifested deep cultural shifts during the decade. The cultural and institutional landscape for Western theological discourse changed as well, with a more civil and latent, but still visible, turmoil that continues today. Lindbeck, Burrell, and Hauerwas all resisted the new landscape for pursuing their craft, even as the majority of theologians and the church assimilated to the new intellectual and institutional backdrop of theological discourse.

In his recent book *A Secular Age*, Charles Taylor describes this 1960s "cultural revolution" as "an individuating revolution." The new cultural framework emphasized "expressive individualism," a form of life that finds its historical origins in late eighteenth-century Romanticism. He writes, "Intellectual and artistic elites have been searching for the authentic way of living or expressing themselves through the nineteenth century. What is new is that this kind of self-orientation seems to have become a mass phenomenon."[35] Social scientists have recognized the shift in the behavior, purpose, and language of those who gather in churches, a shift that occurred as a result of the 1960s.[36] We have sometimes failed to appreciate how this same cultural shift also altered professional theological discourse.

The Western emphasis on authenticity as a virtue finds its roots in the thought of the eighteenth-century Frenchman Jean-Jacques Rousseau.[37] Authenticity developed as a virtue as the elite class attempted to respond to the deistic view of a cold, mechanical universe. Thinkers saw humanity as cut off from the inner force of nature. They argued that humans participate by nature in a dimension that exceeds the mechanism of Newtonian physics through an inner experience of

35. Taylor, *Secular Age*, 473.
36. See, for instance, the work of Robert Wuthnow, especially *The Restructuring of American Religion* (Princeton: Princeton University Press, 1988).
37. For an excellent discussion of Rousseau and the virtue of authenticity, see Jennifer A. Herdt, *Putting on Virtue: The Legacy of the Splendid Vices* (Chicago: University of Chicago Press, 2008), 283–305.

the human self. As Charles Taylor again states, "It is an inner impulse or conviction which tells us of the importance of our own natural fulfillment and of solidarity with our fellow creatures in theirs."[38]

Within this framework, God "is to be interpreted in terms of what we see striving in nature and finding voice within ourselves"[39]—the naturalizing of the supernatural. Individuals must "make manifest" their inner experience through outward expressions. External authorities must submit to the deeper authority of internal individual/communal expressions of universal nature. Life becomes full only when we "find" this experience within ourselves and fully manifest it through our own particular exterior expressions. "The notion of inner depths is therefore intrinsically linked to our understanding of ourselves as expressive, as articulating an inner source."[40]

This, of course, describes the intellectual and social roots of the rise of Protestant liberal theology among the European elite classes in the late eighteenth and nineteenth centuries. Gary Dorrien argues that in the United States, the basic tenet of the Protestant liberal tradition is that "theology should be based on reason and critically interpreted religious experience, not external authority."[41] Friedrich Schleiermacher had developed his expressivist romanticism to address the "cultural despisers" of religion in late eighteenth-century Germany. The Western cultural framework turned authenticity into a mass phenomenon in the 1960s. The cultural shift therefore provided for a rebirth and expansion of the Protestant liberal theological tradition to include even Roman Catholics.

In the early twentieth century, North American liberal Protestants had built an institutional home within elite seminaries and ecclesial educational institutions that, despite appearances

---

38. Charles Taylor, *Sources of the Self: The Making of Modern Identity* (Cambridge: Cambridge University Press, 1989), 369–70.

39. Ibid., 371.

40. Ibid., 390.

41. Gary Dorrien, *The Making of American Liberal Theology*, vol. 3, *Crisis, Irony, and Postmodernity* (Louisville: Westminster John Knox, 2006), 1.

to the contrary, had never been replaced. Inherent liberal commitments always lay within the so-called neo-orthodoxy of mid-
century North America.[42] After the 1960s Protestant liberals
reemerged to anchor theological discourse again in critically
assessed human experience or in the political struggle of various
oppressed, impoverished, or "marginalized" groups.[43]

The explicit reemergence of liberal theology and the emergence of political theologies undercut the advances in ecumenicity that the World Council of Churches had experienced
from the end of the "War to End All Wars" through Vatican II.
Theological discourse fragmented as theologians expressed and
defined the nature of authentic experiences of God. Churches
followed, with various constituencies updating the church's
language to express authentic transcendental experiences of
long-suppressed demographic/interest groups or to fit new
ontological systems, such as process metaphysics. Accepting "pluralism" within traditions became the order of the
day, whereas moving across traditions to discover suppressed
commonalities of faith and order violated the imagination of
a culture of authenticity. Ecumenicity returned to the early
twentieth-century mantra "doctrine divides; service unites,"
which was now expressed in liberationist terms. By 1991, the
World Council of Churches adopted an official doctrinal stance

---

42. Dorrien writes,

> My reading also accentuates the common liberal commitments of Niebuhr,
> Bennett, and Tillich, even as it describes their powerful critiques of liberal
> idealism and rationalism and emphasizes the key differences between Niebuhr
> and Tillich. In their positions on authority, method, and various doctrines,
> and in the spirit of their thinking, Niebuhr, Bennett, and Tillich belonged
> to the liberal tradition even as they insisted that liberal theology was wrong
> to sacralize idealism, wrong to regard reason as inherently redemptive, and
> wrong to suppose that good religion must extinguish its mythical impulses.
> (Dorrien, *Making of American Liberal Theology*, vol. 2, *Idealism, Realism,
> and Modernity 1900–1950* [Louisville: Westminster John Knox, 2003], 9–10)

43. See Dorrien, *Making of American Liberal Theology*, vol. 3. In evangelicalism,
the 1960s and early 1970s witnessed the development of the church growth movement,
which employed the same "kernel-and-husk" analogy as used in Protestant liberalism
and in John XXIII's opening speech of Vatican II. For the Protestant liberal roots of
the church growth theology, see David F. Wells, *God in the Wasteland: The Reality
of Truth in a Land of Fading Dreams* (Grand Rapids: Eerdmans, 1994), esp. 68–87.

to embrace "pluralism" in its effort to work for an invisible unity of the church.[44]

After a century of movement toward visible reconciliation in the church, the beginning of the twenty-first century witnessed a renewed fragmentation even *within* traditional ecclesial communions. Different ethics and politics within common historical traditions generated polemics that eerily reached the stridency of sixteenth-century Protestant/Catholic discourses. One group's authenticity represented another group's moral failure and vice versa. Authenticity in theological language was assumed to be a good, and any thought that might contest authenticity was liable to misunderstanding and resistance.[45] In such a situation, the visible unity of the church (which ought to be grounded in a common apostolic faith, practice, and order) becomes at best a secondary concern and at worst, a hegemonic, totalitarian imposition that threatens the pluralism that authenticity demands. The concern for the visible catholicity of the church that led to and was embraced by Vatican II becomes not merely wrongheaded, but unintelligible.

Lindbeck, Burrell, and Hauerwas all expressly reject authenticity as a key virtue within theology, both in individualist and communal forms. They work within the authority of tradition of the "Great Church" to attempt to overcome the tragic fragmentation of the church. Their projects are not reactionary ones that reject any good in the culture of authenticity, however. Rather they continue, each in their own way, the deeper program of the theological and pastoral renewal of the church by working for the visible unity of the church catholic. They work within the tradition of the *nouvelle théologie* in which creation finds its beginning, sustenance, and end in God and thus, in which the

44. For analyses of the recent history of the World Council of Churches, see Michael Kinnamon, *The Vision of the Ecumenical Movement and How It Has Been Impoverished by Its Friends* (St. Louis: Chalice, 2003); and Carl E. Braaten and Robert W. Jenson, eds., *In One Body through the Cross: The Princeton Proposal for Christian Unity* (Grand Rapids: Eerdmans, 2003).

45. As Jennifer Herdt has astutely observed, "When authenticity is prized, imitating an external model can be seen as falsifying oneself" (*Putting on Virtue*, 6).

theological task is to describe how all things find their end in God. In this eschatological hope, witnessed to in Christ, they continue the concomitant ecumenical commitment to working toward a visible unity of the church. Their theological work presupposes the embodied context of the church so that the church's visible unity might witness to the eternal peaceableness of the Triune God. They seek to salvage the integrity of the witness of the church despite its failures. The task is undertaken not for the church's own enclosed identity, but for the sake of a world torn apart by various incommensurable expressions of human authenticity that can be resolved only by violence.[46]

To do so, however, meant that Lindbeck, Burrell, and Hauerwas not only had to move against underlying cultural dynamics; they also had to face the institutionalizing of the shift to the "culture of authenticity" in the movement of graduate theological formation from church-based institutions to state-sponsored ones. The tectonic plates of history, culture, and institutions had empowered a movement toward the visible unity of the church in the years leading up to the 1960s. The plates now provided considerable resistance for the continuation and advancement of such a program.

"Purely Secular Ends": The Supreme Court and the Institutionalization of "Religious Studies"

Corresponding institutional shifts in North America supported the movement toward a "culture of authenticity" and

---

46. We can see the relationship between the ecclesiology of the postliberals and Vatican II in George Lindbeck's analysis of the relationship between church and mission arising out of the council. Lindbeck writes,

"Church and mission" is handled as a single topic because, according to one strong strain of thought at the Council, "church *is* mission." This means that its essence is to be a sacramental sign or witness to God's saving work in all that it is and does. It exercises this witness or missionary function in its *diakonia* or secular service of the world . . . , its *leitourgia* or worship of God . . . , and its *koinonia* or communal unity expressed both interpersonally and in institutional structures . . . and in common faith and dogma. (George Lindbeck, *The Future of Roman Catholic Theology: Vatican II—Catalyst for Change* [Philadelphia: Fortress, 1969], 5) the democratization of Romantic expressivism in the 1960s. Conservatives have consistently bemoaned the expressivist cultural morals that accompanied this "triumph of the therapeutic" in the 1960s. Ironically, however, American conservatism in the 1960s advocated a laissez-faire, free-market capitalism that itself depended upon the expressivist moral formation of unfettered personal desires.[47] Within a space of fifteen years, the economics that earlier North American conservatives had rejected became the sine qua non of the new conservative movement.[48]

A massive corresponding shift in the institutional theological formation of North Americans also took place in the 1960s. Since the medieval era, Western Christians had located the advanced theological formation of the church within the Western university. This tradition survived the Reformation and (particularly in Protestantism) the rise of the modern research university.[49] The pan-evangelical Protestantism of North American culture reached even into the formation of undergraduates in

47. For capitalism as a "technology of unfettered desire," see Daniel M. Bell Jr., *Liberation Theology after the End of History: The Refusal to Cease Suffering* (London: Routledge, 2001).

48. One can watch this movement within American conservatism through the life of someone like Richard Weaver, a member of what has been called the Southern Agrarian movement. In his "conservative classic," *Ideas Have Consequences* (Chicago: University of Chicago Press, 1948), Weaver criticizes capitalism and its northern industrial base; yet by the late 1950s to early 1960s he had radically liberalized his conservatism in interaction with Chicago scholars like Milton Friedman. According to George H. Nash, by this time he gave a "rousing defense of the American economic system."

> An economy rooted in freedom, incentives, and initiative, he proclaimed, had rewarded Americans with the best standard of living in the world. Capitalism—yes, capitalism—had produced an incomparable cornucopia of plenty. Weaver exhorted his listeners not to feel guilty or defensive about the material achievements of their capitalist system. A society founded upon freedom of enterprise, he averred, was a natural product of unchanging human nature. (George H. Nash, "The Influence of Ideas Have Consequences on the Conservative Intellectual Movement in America," in *Steps towards Restoration: The Consequences of Richard Weaver's Ideas*, ed. Ted J. Smith III [Wilmington, DE: Intercollegiate Studies Institute, 1998], 105)

49. For the role of Protestantism and its subordination to state interests in the founding of the modern *Wissenschaften* university at the University of Berlin, see Thomas Albert Howard, *Protestant Theology and the Making of the Modern German University* (Oxford: Oxford University Press, 2006).

state institutions in the early years of the twentieth century. Private ecclesially-based mainline Protestant universities persisted as vital institutions in North America into the middle of the twentieth century. The task for the graduate formation of pastors and future pastors fell largely to divinity schools connected to private universities.

Significant social shifts began in the late nineteenth century. As part of a struggle for control of American society, "activist secularizers" found support in a group of Protestant liberal church leaders that sought to wrest control of American institutions from a previously dominant orthodox "Protestant establishment."[50] After initial forays into the Protestant seminaries, "second generation liberals . . . took over America's elite divinity schools" in the early twentieth century from the Reformed Protestant Orthodox elite who had previously governed such institutions.[51] Curricular changes soon followed. Near the time when moral philosophy capstone classes fell out of the state university's undergraduate curriculum, private colleges began "Departments of Religion" so that early catechetical classes might be taught "in an academically respectable manner."[52] Underneath the undergraduate and graduate curriculum, however, the categories of Protestant divinity schools still determined what the faculty taught and students studied.

The professors who taught and conducted research for these institutions came largely from church-related private universities with attached divinity schools. Two associations provided the guild context for academic discussion: the Society of Biblical Literature (founded in 1880) and the National Association of Biblical Instructors (founded in 1909 as the Association of Biblical Instructors in American Colleges and Secondary Schools). "Nonsectarian" Protestant thought, with an emphasis on the

50. See Christian Smith's introduction in *The Secular Revolution: Power, Interests, and Conflict in the Secularization of American Public Life*, ed. Christian Smith (Berkeley: University of California Press, 2003), 1–96.

51. Dorrien, *Making of American Liberal Theology*, 2:1.

52. D. G. Hart, *The University Gets Religion: Religious Studies in American Higher Education* (Baltimore: Johns Hopkins University Press, 1999), 10.

role of the Bible in Western civilization, supported democratic American institutions. In the United States, a type of "religious communitarianism" held church and state together for a sense of national culture and mission within U.S. institutions of higher education.[53]

In the 1960s this whole institutional matrix changed, and we can attribute the shift to judicial rulings in the United States. At the undergraduate level, academic engagement of the theological tradition of the church catholic lost its connection to Christian practice; higher education moved toward providing a religious understanding to help students choose their own religious values. College administrators became concerned that there was an "imminent danger that government aid to 'sectarian' colleges and universities would be declared unconstitutional. This was directly relevant to the trustee question because the kind of formal control exercised over an educational institution by a religious organization was one indicatory of sectarianism or its absence."[54] These fears materialized in a 1966 Maryland court ruling denying state grants to three colleges (two Roman Catholic and one Methodist) because of their "sectarian" nature.[55] Such legal threats to the financial stability of church-related colleges and universities no doubt aided a shift from teaching theology, church history, and the Scriptures from the social context of the church to teaching them in the supposedly more

---

53. William T. Cavanaugh writes,
>The Supreme Court's use of the myth of religious violence has never been a response to empirical fact as much as it has been a useful narrative that has been produced by and has helped to produce consent to certain changes in the American social order. Stories of the inherent danger and divisiveness of religion helped to facilitate a shift from a predominant religious communitarianism to a predominant secular individualism in American jurisprudence and American culture. To recognize this shift is not necessarily to imply nostalgia for the previous regime. (William T. Cavanaugh, *The Myth of Religious Violence: Secular Ideology and the Roots of Modern Conflict* [New York: Oxford University Press, 2009], 194)

54. Philip Gleason, *Contending with Modernity: Catholic Higher Education in the Twentieth Century* (Oxford: Oxford University Press, 1995), 315.

55. See Richard Preville, "Catholic Colleges, the Courts, and the Constitution: A Tale of Two Cases," *Church History* 58 (1989): 197–210.

objective context of "religion." The rulings thereby encouraged
the professionalization and secularization of the "religious studies" curriculum in most mainline Protestant and many Roman
Catholic colleges and universities. As Douglas Sloan describes
the situation, "By the end of 1969, along its entire front, the
major twentieth-century engagement of the Protestant church
with American higher education had collapsed, and its forces
were in rout."[56]

The legal threat to these so-called sectarian institutions
affected private church-related college administrators and
trustees—those who represented the church constituencies for
the oversight of the institutions that their congregations had
founded and supported. This weakened the "balance of pow-
ers" when the United States Supreme Court shifted the locus for
graduate study, and the norms for undergraduate study, from
Protestant seminaries to state universities.

The Supreme Court opinion issued the crucial decision in
the case of the School District of Abington Township, Pennsylvania, et al. versus Schempp et al. (1963).[57] The case had nothing to do with higher education (state universities had largely
avoided the constitutional issues by prohibiting academic discourses that raised theological issues). The case involved a
state law that mandated reading ten verses of Scripture and
reciting the Lord's Prayer as part of the opening exercises in
the Pennsylvania public schools. Justice Clark wrote the "opinion of the court" that argued that such a practice violated the

---

56. Douglas Sloan, *Faith and Knowledge: Mainline Protestantism and American
Higher Education* (Louisville: Westminster John Knox, 1994), 206. The same phe-
nomenon occurred in many Roman Catholic institutions of higher education. Philip
Gleason writes,

> Although the dust has still not fully settled, it was clear from an early date
> that the old ideological structure of Catholic higher education, which was
> already under severe strain, had been swept away entirely. As institutions,
> most Catholic colleges and universities weathered the storm. But institutional
> survival in the midst of ideological collapse had left them uncertain of their
> identity. That situation still prevails. (*Contending with Modernity*, 305)

57. All quotations from the case are taken from Abington School Dist. v. Schempp,
374 U.S. 203 (1963), available at http://caselaw.lp.findlaw.com/scripts/getcase.pl?court
=US&vol=374&invol=203.

"neutrality" of the government toward "religion." The justice, however, argued that the decision did not advocate a "'religion of secularism' in the sense of opposing or showing hostility to religion." As evidence he offered that "it might well be said that one's education is not complete without a study of comparative religion or the history of religion and its relationship to the advancement of civilization. It certainly may be said that the Bible is worthy of study for its literary and historic qualities. Nothing we have said here indicates that such study of the Bible or of religion, when presented objectively as part of a secular program of education, may not be effected consistently with the First Amendment."

In a concurring "opinion," Justice Brennan explicitly strayed from the case to advocate for state-sponsored teaching of religion for "purely secular ends"; theology, with its "purely sectarian ends," of course, was not even considered. Justice Brennan's opinion deserves an extended quotation:

> While it is not, of course, appropriate for this Court to decide questions not presently before it, I venture to suggest that religious exercises in the public schools present a unique problem. For not every involvement of religion in public life violates the Establishment Clause. Our decision in these cases does not clearly forecast anything about the constitutionality of other types of interdependence between religious and other public institutions. . . . Nothing in the Establishment Clause forbids the application of legislation having purely secular ends in such a way as to alleviate burdens upon the free exercise of an individual's religious beliefs. . . . The holding of the Court today plainly does not foreclose teaching about the Holy Scriptures or about the differences between religious sects in classes in literature or history. Indeed, whether or not the Bible is involved, it would be impossible to teach meaningfully many subjects in the social sciences or the humanities without some mention of religion. To what extent, and at what points in the curriculum, religious materials should be cited are matters which the courts ought to entrust very largely to the experienced officials who superintend our Nation's public schools.

Though this judgment was admittedly not "appropriate," scholars quickly jumped on Brennan's suggestion to establish the
patronage of the state for the study of the Christian tradition,
now "having purely secular ends" as a particular type of object
of study within the larger genre of "religion."

Major assumptions undergirded Brennan's suggestion that both
arose out of and contributed to the revolution of the culture of
authenticity. First, and most obvious, the suggestion presupposes
the empirical reality of a discrete realm of "religion" that exists
within humans that we can readily, even if with difficulty, separate
from a "secular" realm. To study "religion" is to study a Romantic inner expressive realm outside and opposed to the bounds of
purely secular reason that nonetheless leaves physical, material,
and social traces in the world. After decades of methodological
hand-wringing, however, prominent scholars within "religious
studies" have decried the empirical vacuity of the concept, except
as a term that masks the colonial interests of liberal expressivist
Protestant theology.[58] William Cavanaugh has recently argued that

> there is no such thing as a transhistorical or transcultural "re-
> ligion" that is essentially separate from politics. Religion has a
> history, and what counts as religion and what does not in any
> given context depends on different configurations of power and
> authority. . . . The attempt to say that there *is* a transhistori-
> cal and transcultural concept of religion that is separable from
> secular phenomena *is itself* part of a particular configuration of
> power, that of the modern, liberal nation-state as it developed in
> the West. In this context, religion is constructed as transhistori-
> cal, transcultural, essentially interior, and essentially distinct
> from public, secular rationality.[59]

The concept of "religion" serves to marginalize theological traditions that have historical origins from long before a liberal

58. See, for instance, Hart, *University Gets Religion*; see also Timothy Fitzgerald,
The Ideology of Religious Studies (Oxford: Oxford University Press, 2003); and Rus-
sell T. McCutcheon, *Manufacturing Religion: The Discourse on Sui Generis Religion
and the Politics of Nostalgia* (Oxford: Oxford University Press, 1997).

59. Cavanaugh, *Myth of Religious Violence*, 9.

polity arose. As Cavanaugh again writes, "Loyalty to one's religion is private in origin and therefore optional; loyalty to the secular nation-state is what unifies us and is not optional."[60] The institutional domination of "religious studies" within North American higher education works to shift loyalties of students and professors to the "purely secular ends" of the nation-state through the naturalness of studying something called "religious expressions"—the empirical manifestations of some internal human experience. In the process, the linguistic backdrop diminishes the same students' (and professors') loyalties to particular embodied theological institutions in favor of advocating for a student's own self-expression.

Second, an anthropology remains implicit within the discourse of "religious studies" that contributes toward the end of authenticity. Michael Sandel has persuasively argued that the court's decisions in matters of "religion" presuppose an "unencumbered self"—that is, a self that is prior to any particular good it pursues, ahistorical, and ultimately autonomous except for its own right to chose its own goods.[61] Such a conception of the self renders churches, synagogues, or mosques voluntary associations built upon the authenticity of human choice to express inner values in line with historical communities. The unencumbered self cannot account for what the church or synagogue or mosque must be, what Sandel calls a "constitutive community" that engages "the identity as well as the interests of the participants, and so implicate[s] its members in a citizenship more thoroughgoing than the unencumbered self can know."[62] Further, "it fails to capture those loyalties and responsibilities whose moral force consists partly in the fact that living by them is inseparable from understanding ourselves as the particular person we are."[63] Religious studies

60. Ibid., 121.
61. Michael J. Sandel, "The Procedural Republic and the Unencumbered Self," *Political Theory* 12 (1984), 86.
62. Ibid., 87.
63. Michael J. Sandel, "Freedom of Conscience or Freedom of Choice?" in *Articles of Faith, Articles of Peace: The Religious Liberty Clauses and the American Public*

for "purely secular ends" effectively accomplishes the end that Brennan states. It "depreciates the claims of religion and fails to respect persons bound by duties they have not chosen."[64] Rather than establishing embodied historic traditions that refuse to divorce faith and reason, the court-inspired move naturalized "religion" as the historical manifestation of nonrational internal experiences of humans. The court's judgment, in its application and its presuppositions, contributed to the theological expressivism that underlay the revolution to a culture of authenticity.

State universities warmly received the decision. The expansion of state institutions of higher education in the 1960s afforded the opportunity to found new departments of "religious studies" for graduate as well as undergraduate formation.[65] The academic guild structure immediately changed to institutionalize Brennan's suggestion. A self-study committee of the National Association of Biblical Instructors recommended that the organization change its name to "The American Academy of Religion," which it did in 1964. Although it was not until 1979 that the American Council of Learned Societies recognized the academic legitimacy of the AAR, "religion" rather than theology framed academic graduate training; the state rather than the church or synagogue or mosque became the "constituency" for the discourse. As D. G. Hart observes,

> Religious studies' professionalization came at a great price. Not only did this process require the abandonment of the devotional, ethical, and cultural purposes that religious studies founders believed to be essential to their academic work, but the professionalization of the field also left religious studies without an identity. Stripped of the pious and social grounds for studying religion, religious studies could not produce a set of compelling intellectual reasons for its place in the university.[66]

Philosophy, ed. James Davison Hunter and Os Guinness (Washington, DC: Brookings Institution, 1990), 77.

64. Ibid., 92.

65. For a narrative of this history, see Hart, University Gets Religion.

66. Ibid., 202–3.

The only "compelling intellectual reason" may be to serve the "purely secular ends" of the nation-state with a population formed to function in a culture of authenticity. Theological discourse that presupposed or worked for the unity of the church became unintelligible within this institutional matrix. One might find in state universities the study of comparative religion, but one will not find the promotion of the visible unity of the church catholic.

The results of the court opinions became quickly embedded institutionally. "Religious studies" exploded as an undergraduate discipline on American campuses. State programs provided the models for private colleges and universities, both church-related and non-church-related. Faculty revised their curricula in ways that administrators could support in order to ameliorate charges of "sectarianism" that might threaten state grants. State-run graduate programs quickly displaced the elite Protestant seminaries that had formed the previous generation of faculty. The changing institutional matrix transformed disciplines as graduate students were socialized into fields of study that were indirectly established by Brennan's inappropriate suggestion. Seminaries attempted to sustain their academic credibility by incorporating the state-formed categories into their formation of graduate students, for those pursuing both academic and parish responsibilities. Seminaries themselves, to a greater or lesser degree, became "graduate schools of religion."

The whole disciplinary matrix for the study of the Christian tradition changed as earlier disciplines faded from view with their place usurped by new discourses. For instance, before the 1960s "patristics" named the academic study of early Christian history and texts. As a discipline, it arose out of the nineteenth-century English Oxford movement that sought to retrieve early church discourse and practices for the renewal of the church. In the new institutional setting of the state, scholars named the study of early Christian history and texts "early Christian studies." "Patristics" became "taken as a sign of ecclesiasticism, maleness, and 'orthodoxy,' from which some scholars wished to dissociate themselves."[67] Through this dissociation, scholars could explore alternative expressions of inner human experiences that history had supposedly irrationally suppressed. They thereby benefited from the patronage of the state to support their studies and subsequent careers.

State patronage gave "religious studies" the impulse needed to become an incredible academic growth industry. Elizabeth Clark summarizes the amazing statistical change:

> Although graduate education was slow to develop in the United States . . . , fifty-two PhD programmes in religion were in operation by 1970, aided by a 1963 Supreme Court ruling that granted public educational institutions the right to teach "about" religion. Between 1964 and 1968, the number of graduate students in religion jumped from 7,383 to 12,620, a rate of growth exceeding that of any other academic discipline. From this time onward, graduate students in religion frequently chose programmes in nondenominational departments of religious studies within university settings. This trend was also present in some of the newer British universities.[68]

With the expressivist cultural shift, the encouragement of their professors, and the financial and social patronage of the state, the "choice" of graduate students to move from the "confines" of the church to the "freedom" of the state for their advanced studies of the Christian tradition must have seemed self-evident.

The dissemination of the "Welch Report" in 1971 embedded the institutionalization of state-sponsored "religious studies" even more deeply into American higher education.[69] Claude Welch, then dean of Berkeley's Graduate Theological Union, directly engaged the new disciplinary situation arising from Brennan's suggestion: "Graduate studies in religion, formerly

---

67. Elizabeth A. Clark, "From Patristics to Early Christian Studies," in *The Oxford Handbook of Early Christian Studies*, ed. Susan Ashbrook Harvey and David G. Hunter (Oxford: Oxford University Press, 2008), 14.

68. Ibid., 15.

69. See Claude Welch, *Graduate Education in Religion: A Critical Appraisal* (Missoula: University of Montana Press, 1971).

carried on almost entirely in or in close association with theological schools, have also been rapidly changing. Numerous
PhD and master's programs have been established in universities having no theological schools. Some older programs have
been radically restructured."[70] The report served to order the
vast changes in the academic study of the Christian tradition.
It recorded the changes statistically, provided rationales for the
changes after the fact, and offered recommendations for the
longer-term integration of religious studies within American
higher education based upon maintaining state patronage.

The report sought to distance undergraduate education
farther from its historic ecclesial location by using "academic
graduate schools" (i.e., religious-studies programs) rather than
"professional schools" (seminaries and rabbinical schools) as
the norm for undergraduate programs.[71] It encouraged study
of non-Jewish and non-Christian traditions and a social-
scientific, rather than historical and textual, approach to its
topics. It also recommended that graduate study be removed
from the context of seminaries and placed into university
programs.[72] Perhaps most interestingly, it explicitly articulated

70. Ibid., vii–viii.

71. Welch writes, "A new integration is needed between graduate study in religion
and undergraduate studies. Such integration is made possible by the expansion and
the improvement in quality of undergraduate academic programs of religious studies.
It is necessitated by the growing independence of graduate studies from the work of
the professional schools" (ibid., 4).

72. Ibid., 4–7. These recommendations represent very intentional shifts away from
the historical, institutional basis for the graduate study of the theological crafts, as
the statistics recorded the historical anchorage of graduate studies in the Protestant-
related seminaries:

> Eight institutions, for example, produced two-thirds of the approximately
> 2,250 PhDs in religion given between 1952 and 1969. There were Yale (with
> 308 PhDs), Boston (288), Chicago (230), Columbia (167, with which should
> probably be associated 138 ThDs at Union Theological Seminary), Duke
> (158), Harvard (126 plus 78 ThDs), Drew (123), and Vanderbilt (108). . . .
> There is a striking concentration of graduate religious studies in a handful of
> theological school faculties that either are an integral part of the university
> or work in close association with an adjacent university. (Ibid., 39)

The report thereby notices that the severing between the church and the universities had already occurred at the graduate level. Now the committee sought to make
this process complete at the undergraduate level.

the "purely secular ends" for oversight and assessment of the programs:

> Effective organs are required for representing the academic study of religion to the several publics to which it is responsible, in particular to the civic community. The Council on the Study of Religion and its constituent professional societies should particularly be encouraged to undertake the task of more adequate interpretation of the study of religion and theology both to governmental agencies and to other academic associations.[73]

The report recommended that graduate theological studies develop mechanisms to report to "government agencies" to oversee the churches', synagogues', and mosques' theological learning! Patronage always comes with a price.

In retrospect one discovers that the report's recommendations legitimated changes that were already well underway. Brennan's suggestion inadvertently became the most influential theological text in North America for the last half of the twentieth century and on into the foreseeable future. The significance of this story for us is that the first-generation postliberals sustained the earlier, traditional, ecclesially-based program for theology in the face of this institutional shift. They intellectually, and to many minds successfully, challenged the philosophical and anthropological presuppositions upon which the institutional change was based. Their very agendas opposed the state patronage that had quickly formed the guild of "religious studies" in the 1960s. By conducting theology within the embodied historical tradition of the church for the very nonsecular ends of the catholicity of the church, the first-generation postliberals endangered the newly established state patronage for scholars from within the academy itself.

Lindbeck, Burrell, and Hauerwas refused to accept the theological suggestion of Judge Brennan at multiple levels and thus worked against the grain of the changing institutional matrix of the North American religious studies academic formation. Each

73. Ibid., 7.

of the theologians interviewed below had their chief academic formation before this institutional change occurred. They have vigorously worked from within the church and for the future of the church's witness; they deny philosophically the existence of an "unencumbered self." And they conducted their research, writing, and formation of graduate students within explicitly ecclesial educational contexts—the divinity schools of Yale and Duke, and the Department of Theology of the University of Notre Dame. By critiquing the institutional change from within and continuing academic engagement and formation of graduate students for the sake of the historic faith given to the saints, Lindbeck, Burrell, and Hauerwas resisted the interlocked cultural and academic institutional shifts. Instead they sustained a constituency in the church for theological formation and, out of their difference from the culture and its institutions, provided critical intellectual engagement publicly in service to the wider society.

In order to keep to their task, these three thinkers innovatively drew upon the intellectual strength of two philosophical traditions that the culture of authenticity and institutionalized departments of religious studies (and their theological understudies) had abandoned as culturally, intellectually, and theologically unhelpful. These traditions are Thomistic philosophical theology and contemporary Anglo-American analytic linguistic philosophy. By tacking against the wind, Lindbeck, Burrell, and Hauerwas have implemented a fruitful program for thought and life.

Is God Dead? Analytic Thomism as a Response to the Problem of Theological Language

On April 8, 1966, *Time* magazine ran its famous "Is God Dead?" cover. The article chronicles the then-new (a)theological works that caught public attention during the flux of the 1960s. Academically and culturally, theological language formed the crux of the matter: How does the language of God work? What work does it do, if any? As stated in the article, "What unites the various contemporary approaches to the problem of God is the conviction that the primary question has become not what God is, but how men are justified in using the word."[74] Theologians left unfinished the task of working for the visible unity of the church; they instead sought to engage the cultural and secularist philosophical backdrop of the earlier twentieth century. Capturing the mood of the time, they sought a language that could maintain the "gospel" without God: "The contemporary world appears so biased against metaphysics that any attempt to find philosophical equivalents for God may well be doomed to failure."[75] When in Rome, do as the Romans do.

The "secular theologians" engaged a philosophical tradition that most Protestant and Catholic theologians had largely disregarded in the previous decades. Analyzing language (how it works, what it does, and how to distinguish meaningful language from nonsense) had dominated, and still dominates, twentieth-century Anglo-American philosophical thought. The secular theologians of the 1960s accepted the results of the logical positivists. These philosophers argued that language is only meaningful if it has a reference that humans can empirically verify or at least falsify; all other language is nonsense.

The "verificationist" view of language represented a position deeply embedded in the post-Enlightenment Western tradition, one that sees language's role as primarily designative. Charles Taylor describes this tradition: "We could explain a sign or word having meaning by pointing to what it designates, in a broad sense, that is, what it can be used to refer to in the world, and what it can be used to say about that thing. . . . On this view, we give the meaning of a sign or a word by pointing to the things or relations that can be used to refer or talk about."[76] Since the Triune God obviously is not an empirical object in the world, theologians who accepted this position attempted to develop

---

74. John T. Elson, "Theology: Toward a Hidden God," *Time*, April 8, 1966, available at http://www.time.com/time/magazine/article/0,9171,835309-1,00.html.

75. Ibid.

76. Charles Taylor, "Language and Human Nature," in *Human Agency and Language: Philosophical Papers I* (Cambridge: Cambridge University Press, 1985), 218.

"the secular meaning of the gospel" without the purported nonsense of any language of God.

This secularist position may seem to contradict our earlier argument concerning the Romantic, expressivist institutionalization of theology that arose from the cultural and institutional shifts of the 1960s. In one way, it does. The analytic philosophical tradition was perceived as a theological dead end.[77] Theological training moved away from the linguistic philosophical tradition of Anglo-American philosophy departments. Analytic philosophy seemed solely the realm of scientism, "the doctrine that *only* the methods of the natural sciences give rise to knowledge."[78] Theology is obviously not a "natural science," and the scientistic agenda seemingly closed off the analytic philosophical tradition to theologians. More pressing, theology seemingly had no intellectual basis for speaking about God and all things related to God.

A second tradition of language, however, also existed within the Western cultural heritage, one with roots much older than the "designative" tradition. Charles Taylor calls this tradition an "expressive tradition" of language. In this tradition, in language "something is expressed, when it is embodied in such a way as to be made manifest. And 'manifest' must be taken here in a strong sense. Something is manifest when it is directly available for all to see. . . . What expression manifests can *only* be manifest in expression."[79]

Theologians went to an indirect, expressive view of language to find a basis for a "theological language" that could still "designate" God, even if indirectly via the self or experience. The expressivist theological tradition arose out of and fed back into the 1960s' cultural emphasis on Romantic expressivism. God

77. See R. R. Reno, "Theology's Continental Captivity," *First Things*, April 2006, available at http://www.firstthings.com/article/2007/01/theology8217s-continental -captivity---18. For a wonderful engagement with analytic philosophy for its importance to understand theological language, see D. Stephen Long, *Speaking of God: Theology, Language, and Truth* (Grand Rapids: Eerdmans, 2009).

78. Avrum Stroll, *Twentieth-Century Analytic Philosophy* (New York: Columbia University Press, 2000), 1.

79. Taylor, "Language and Human Nature," 218–19.

was not an external, empirical object in the world; theologians saw "expression" making manifest the experience or presence of God internally in human beings. Theological language became understood as projective from the self. Good theology projected the self or experience authentically.

Via the concept of "religion," theological language thereby had an empirical basis for its academic work: "religious traditions" both expressed *and* designated inner experiences within the self and the communities that constructed that self. Theologians left scientism and analytic verificationism, with its problematizing of language of God, intact. They also left themselves with only the resources of the continental philosophical tradition arising out of eighteenth- and nineteenth-century Romanticisms.[80] The analytic exclusion of "God-talk" shared a deep logic with the language of "religion" and the institutionalization of "religious studies" to feed into the resurgence of the cultural Protestant liberal theological program, even as this program bled over into Roman Catholicism and American Protestant evangelicalism. "Religion" at least afforded a mediating language to speak of God in a "postmetaphysical" world. This seemed like the only option the institutional framework gave theologians in which to work.

We must appreciate—or at least mourn—the intellectual irony of the whole situation. The very philosophical position that 1960s American secular "theologians" accepted as necessary to remain relevant to the intellectual framework of the world had already been largely abandoned by Anglo-American analytic philosophers. By the end of the 1940s analytic philosophers had dismissed "verificationist" positions because "every precise formulation of it had been decisively refuted."[81] Anglo-

---

80. This includes contemporary theological engagement with thinkers such as Foucault and Derrida. Charles Taylor places these thinkers in a tradition of what he calls "the immanent counter-Enlightenment" arising out of Romanticism. See *Secular Age*, 599–600.

81. "The argument is no stronger than verificationism in general, which by 1949, when *The Concept of Mind* was published, had been abandoned by its main proponents, the logical positivists, for the simple reason that every precise formulation of it

American philosophers had begun, instead, to engage the later thought of the Austrian-born Cambridge philosopher, Ludwig Wittgenstein. Scott Soames describes two "leading ideas" that engage analytic philosophy based upon the Wittgensteinian text:

> The first was that philosophical problems are due solely to the misuse of language. Thus, the job of the philosopher is not to construct elaborate theories to solve philosophical problems, but to expose the linguistic confusions that fooled us into thinking there were genuine problems to be solved in the first place. The second leading idea is that meaning itself—the key to progress in philosophy—was *not* to be studied from a theoretical or abstract scientific perspective. Rather than constructing general theories of meaning, philosophers were supposed to attend to subtle aspects of language use, and to show how misuse of certain words leads to philosophical perplexity and confusion.[82]

Academic theologians had presupposed an abandoned philosophical position against which their Romantic expressivism reacted as it set itself up as its dialectical opposition. Even as theologians divided over choosing between secularist atheological positions or "authentic" religious/theological positions emanating from an expressivist self, a third vein remained open for discourse—one that could explain how language of God worked differently than language about the world, but still meaningfully. Such a vein could simultaneously serve the ecumenical purpose of working for the visible unity of the church. It consisted of the reappropriation of the theology of Thomas Aquinas through the tools of analytic philosophy.

Lindbeck, Burrell, and Hauerwas all engaged the theological ramifications of this third way in startlingly creative, intellectually rigorous, yet profoundly orthodox manners. As the interviews below will show, a crucial text for understanding the background of Lindbeck's, Burrell's, and Hauerwas's work is Victor Preller's *Divine Science and the Science of God: A Reformulation*

---

had been decisively refuted" (Scott Soames, *Philosophical Analysis in the Twentieth Century*, vol. 2, *The Age of Meaning* [Princeton: Princeton University Press, 2003], 98).

82. Ibid., xiii–xiv.

of Thomas Aquinas.[83] Preller reinterpreted Thomas Aquinas's thought through the analytic philosophy of Wilfrid Sellars. He read Aquinas as a type of "linguistic therapist" who instructs readers how to speak well of God and the world in relation to God.[84] Preller showed that analytic philosophy was not an enemy to theological discourse, but, properly used, its ally.

Preller also showed that, at one level, the verificationist criticism of theological language would not have bothered Thomas at all. He showed that, for Thomas, *if* language could designate or refer to God per se, it would not be the Triune God to which it referred, but an idol. Thomas, instead, understood language as functioning in fundamentally different ways depending on whether one spoke of God or creation: we know God as One unknown. Preller's use of theological language was not expressive of an inner experience of the human self. Aquinas shows how theological language works within a conceptual scheme to speak of God and all things in relation to God whereby "expression is the power of a subject; and expressions *manifest* things, and hence essentially refer us to subjects for whom these can be manifest."[85] Epistemology, how one knows, depends upon ontology, what one desires to know. By careful attention to how theological language worked for Thomas, Preller shows that a response to the problem of the language of God was already embedded in the "conceptual scheme" or language of the orthodox Christian tradition.[86]

83. Victor Preller, *Divine Science and the Science of God: A Reformulation of Thomas Aquinas* (1967; repr., Eugene, OR: Wipf and Stock, 2005). It is interesting to note that the prominent American analytic pragmatic philosopher Richard Rorty was a reader of Preller's dissertation.

84. For the common therapeutic attention to the workings of language between Aquinas and Wittgenstein, see the wonderful essay by Joseph Incandela, "Similarities and Synergy: An Augustinian Reading of Aquinas and Wittgenstein," in Stout and MacSwain, *Grammar and Grace*, 20–54.

85. Taylor, "Language and Human Nature," 224.

86. Robert Cathey helpfully connects the "postliberals" to what has been called an "internal realism": "According to my way of framing postliberal theology, assertions of 'justified true beliefs' (religious, scientific, ethical, artistic) always emerge in time out of our communities of inquiry, cultural-linguistic systems, personal life-experiences, and the testimony of others. Even as finite, fallible, temporal, socialized

In the language of John XXIII, Preller opened a discourse that sought to renew the faith through an updating that was simultaneously a return to its classical sources. Though criticized for his reading of Thomas as emphasizing Thomas's negative theology[87]—that what we can know about God is what God is *not*—his work was rightly seen as opening a path to a christological reading of Thomas. Preller wrote:

> *Sacra doctrina* is the action of God who makes himself known. The prime locus of God's act of self-communication is God

truth-tellers, we make these claims about something more than our so-called private states of experience" (Cathey, *God in Postliberal Perspective*, 187). The similarity to Hilary Putnam's position in *Reason, Truth and History* (Cambridge: Cambridge University Press, 1981) is remarkable; Putnam writes,

> The position I have defended is that any choice of a conceptual scheme presupposes values, and the choice of a scheme for describing ordinary interpersonal relations as social facts, not to mention thinking about one's own life plan, involves, among other things, one's *moral* values. One cannot choose a scheme which simply "copies" the facts, because *no* conceptual scheme is a mere "copy" of the world. The notion of truth itself depends for its content on our standards of rational acceptability, and these in turn rest on and presuppose our values. Put schematically and too briefly, I am saying that theory of truth presupposes theory of rationality which in turn presupposes our theory of the good. (215; emphasis in original)

Perhaps, however, one could find a closer position in the careful linguistic reading of Thomas Aquinas given by John P. O'Callaghan, *Thomistic Realism and the Linguistic Turn: Toward a More Perfect Form of Existence* (Notre Dame: University of Notre Dame Press, 2003). O'Callaghan writes,

> Thought is not by nature private, but rather public. But the public is not just the educated or even uneducated speaking public. A better and non-reductive understanding of the sciences under which human beings fall presents an opportunity for developing an authentic philosophical anthropology. Here, perhaps, one can see a deep affinity between Thomist Realism and a certain understanding of Wittgenstein and the Linguistic Turn. For the Thomistic Aristotelian, conceptual functioning on the part of the human animal is naturally ordered toward expression in non-linguistic and linguistic acts alike, forming through these linguistic and non-linguistic acts social and political communities. But like any human act, we can deliberately choose to cut word and deed short of their completion or fulfillment. When we do so, we choose not to flourish as human beings. We choose a less perfect form of existence. (298)

87. See Fergus Kerr, "'Real Knowledge' or 'Enlightened Ignorance': Eric Mascall on the Apophatic Thomisms of Victor Preller and Victor White," in Stout and MacSwain, *Grammar and Grace*, 103–23.

himself—the eternal and immanent expression of his personal intentional state, terminating in the eternal Word. . . . All revelation, however, and thus all *sacra doctrina*, is an extension of the eternal procession of the Word; it is, in theological terminology, the temporal *mission* of the eternal Person. The central historical locus of the temporal mission of the Word of God is the sacred humanity of Christ. Therefore, the prime locus of "speech about God" is *sacra scriptura*, the primary subject of which is Christ. Scripture is itself a created analogue of God's act of self-knowledge as expressed in his Word or inner speech. Conformation of the mind to the intention of sacred scripture effects the conformation of the soul to the Second Person of the Trinity.[88]

Whereas many had followed Barth in reading *Church Dogmatics* against Thomas's *Summa Theologiae*, Preller's analytic, linguistic reading of Thomas ironically opened a way to return to a christocentric Thomism that nonetheless could incorporate a moral theology emphasizing the Christian virtues.[89]

The linguistic turn in reading Aquinas provided one other virtue for theology—it provided a tool for ecumenical progress. Thomas had adopted the medieval "quaestionis" form for his theological work. This consisted of a question, a brief statement of a position, followed by more extensive arguments directly opposing the position just taken, and then the solution, with justification against an opposing position. As Alasdair MacIntyre states,

> To each question the answer produced by Aquinas as a conclusion is no more than and, given Aquinas's method, cannot but be no more than, the best answer reached so far. And hence derives the essential incompleteness. For what Aquinas does is

88. Preller, *Divine Science*, 232–33.
89. One therefore finds common roots between the postliberals and thinkers such as Elizabeth Anscombe and Peter Geach, from whom a vigorous realm of philosophical thought christened "Analytic Thomism" has arisen. See John Haldane, "Analytic Thomism: How We Got Here, Why It Is Worth Remaining and Where We May Go to Next," in *Analytic Thomism: Traditions in Dialogue*, ed. Craig Paterson and Matthew S. Pugh (Burlington, VT: Ashgate, 2006), 303–10. For the relationship between Thomas and analytic philosophy, see also Fergus Kerr, "Aquinas and Analytic Philosophy: Natural Allies?" in *Aquinas in Dialogue: Thomas for the Twenty-First Century*, ed. Jim Fodor and Frederick Christian Bauerschmidt (London: Blackwell, 2004), 119–35.

to summarize on each question the strongest arguments for and against each particular answer which have so far been formulated, drawing upon all the texts and all the strands of developing argument which have informed the traditions which he inherits. . . . But when Aquinas has reached his conclusion, the method leaves open the possibility of a return to that question with some new argument. . . . The narrative of enquiry always points beyond itself with directions drawn from the past, which, so that past itself teaches, will themselves be open to change.[90]

The Thomistic dialectical method allows the reconciliation or reordering of statements through a careful analysis of the workings of language within a particular context. Contemporary advances in linguistic philosophy could help to engage doctrines more therapeutically. Through linguistic philosophy, the quaestionis method permits the possibility that perhaps previous doctrines of the fragmented church, once seen as irreconcilable, may prove reconcilable when seen in their particular conceptual schemes. The past still teaches the present church authoritatively. Theologians, while faithful to their own particular traditions within the church catholic, might work for the visible unity of the church through a type of ecumenical linguistic therapy. Theologians across theological traditions can use such linguistic therapy to clarify similarities and differences.

Lindbeck, Burrell, and Hauerwas all work within the framework of an apophatic and christocentric reading of the Christian tradition through the resources provided by St. Thomas as interpreted with the aid of contemporary analytic philosophy. For them, unlike so much contemporary philosophy and theology, epistemology depends upon ontology. Analytic philosophical tools provide a startling up-to-date restatement of the Christian tradition through a radical return to the sources. The problem of theological language is not "solved" but is overcome through faith that is always already embedded in the use of reason. Coming in the wake of the mid-century progress toward the visible

90. Alasdair MacIntyre, *Three Rival Versions of Moral Enquiry: Encyclopaedia, Genealogy, and Tradition* (Notre Dame: University of Notre Dame Press, 1990), 124–25.

unity of the church that culminated at Vatican II, the work of
Lindbeck, Burrell, and Hauerwas redraws Protestant/Roman
Catholic traditions that render such distinctions problematic
even as it addresses the intellectual conundrums of the secularist
world in which we live.

Conclusion

If the above background is accurate, perhaps what is most remarkable about the thought and lives of George Lindbeck, David
Burrell, and Stanley Hauerwas is that these first-generation
postliberals sustained such a theological program throughout
the last half of the twentieth century while the cultural and
institutional currents in which they worked moved explicitly
against them. One can detect in their stories that they have experienced the ambivalence of their success amid greater failure
in their lives, lives that have refused the disciplinary safety of the
academic guild of religious studies. The historical contingencies
of their own lives played themselves out amid wider currents of
cultural, intellectual, and theological history. They have resisted
assimilative moves in the constant development of their theological programs. They have done so with sufficient intellectual
force and integrity that their agendas, which could otherwise
have been completely lost to the world, have nonetheless been
nurtured and even grown—through their embodied ecclesial
commitments, their writings, and their students. Their stories
are worthy of being preserved, not only separately, but together.

    T. S. Eliot once wrote, "If we take the widest and wisest view
of a Cause, there is no such thing as a Lost Cause because there
is no such thing as a Gained Cause. We fight for lost causes
because we know that our defeat and dismay may be the preface to our successor's victory, though the victory itself will
be temporary; we fight rather to keep something alive than in
the expectation that anything will triumph."[91] If such bellicose

91. T. S. Eliot, "Francis Herbert Bradley," in *Selected Prose of T. S. Eliot*, ed. Frank
Kermode (New York: Harvest Books, 1975), 199–200.

imagery is appropriate for these theologians, this saying is an apt reminder that in our day, any future cultural tectonic shifts that return Christians to their ecumenical roots will result not from the work of humans, but by the work of the God whom we know as One unknown, but who has graciously revealed God's own Triune Self in Jesus Christ by the Holy Spirit. In the meantime, perhaps through remembering such stories and wisdom as these that follow, we can keep something alive that would otherwise be lost.

3

"I Pray That They Might Be One as We Are One"

An Interview with George Lindbeck

In January 2007 George Lindbeck, David Burrell, and Stanley Hauerwas gathered together at Nazarene Theological Seminary in Kansas City, Missouri, where they participated in interviews conducted by John Wright to reflect on their lives, their academic work, and their friendship. The interviews particularly delved into the impact of Vatican II on their lives and thought, and their reflections and contributions on the continued quest for the visible unity of the church catholic.

As the senior scholar, Professor Lindbeck was interviewed first. Professor Lindbeck's adult life was centered at Yale—from his appointment as an instructor at Yale College in 1951 to his retirement as emeritus professor from Yale Divinity School in 1993. Having been raised in China as the son of Lutheran missionaries, Professor Lindbeck exemplifies a depth and irenicism

*of character honed by decades of selfless work in ecumenical
discourses. He stands as a counter-exemplar to trends of the
contemporary intellectual in which "intellectuals have come
to see their careers in capitalistic terms. They seek out market
niches. They compete for attention. They used to regard ideas
as weapons but are now more inclined to regard their ideas as
property."[1] In contrast Professor Lindbeck has often worked
anonymously or as a member of joint working groups to reestablish the visible unity of the church. Such a program, however,
has led him into controversies and polemics as well.[2] His life
witnesses how God can transform a young scholar's concern
to establish a career into the much more difficult task of using
one's intellectual acumen for the glory of God, seen in the witness of the visible body of Christ in the world.[3]*

On His Medieval Studies

I didn't have a passion for medieval studies. It was entirely, so
to speak, a means toward an end. And that end was the study
of contemporary Catholicism. Back in the immediate postwar
period, when I entered graduate studies, the way to become
an expert in contemporary Roman Catholicism was to start

1. David Brooks, *Bobos in Paradise: The New Upper Class and How They Got There* (New York: Simon and Schuster, 2000), 149.

2. Professor Lindbeck was a signatory of the "Hartford Declaration" in 1975, which protested "the loss of a sense of transcendence" that was "debilitating to the church's witness and mission" (Hazel Andrews, "The Hartford Declaration," available at http:// www.philosophy-religion.org/handouts/pdfs/Hartford-Affirmation.pdf). Interestingly, members of the Harvard and University of Chicago Divinity Schools were invited to sign the declaration but refused, perhaps foreshadowing tensions that would arise later with the publication of *The Nature of Doctrine*. Many years later Professor Lindbeck was a signatory with a completely new generation of theologians of the "Princeton Proposal for Christian Unity" (Carl E. Braaten and Robert W. Jenson, eds., *In One Body through the Cross: The Princeton Proposal for Christian Unity* [Grand Rapids: Eerdmans, 2005]). For Professor Lindbeck's defense of the "Princeton Proposal," see George A. Lindbeck, "The Unity We Seek," *Christian Century*, August 9, 2005, 28–31.

3. For other biographical interviews with Mr. Lindbeck, see George Weigel, "Reviewing Vatican II: An Interview with George A. Lindbeck," *First Things*, December 1994, 44–50; "Performing the Faith: An Interview with George Lindbeck," *Christian Century*, November 28, 2006, 28–35.

with the Middle Ages, and specifically with Thomas Aquinas. So really the question is, how did I get interested in studying contemporary Catholicism? And that's a long story. I'll try to abbreviate it.

I think it started very early on hearing my mother talk about certain cousins of mine, that is to say, children of her brother, who had married a Catholic and become a Catholic. So I had six Roman Catholic cousins. There was always a rather strange note that crept into my mother's voice whenever she spoke about them. It was a slightly different tone than when she talked about our other cousins—all of whom I didn't know. We were in China as missionaries; they were thousands of miles away in the United States. When I was eleven years old we went home (or back) to the United States for furlough, and among the things we did was visit these cousins. We all slept in the same room—my brother and I and five male cousins—so the five boys and the two of us slept in the attic in a sort of dormitory set-up. Their habits of going to bed at night were extraordinarily similar to my own. That is to say that they would read a little Scripture, and they would pray silently, kneeling at their bedside, and then we'd all go to bed and say good night to each other.

The parish that they belonged to was a German Catholic parish, which like many German Catholic parishes had been influenced by long competition with Lutherans back in Germany, and so it was much more scripturally oriented. They had been taught in the parish that they should read the Scriptures and so on and so forth, which would not have happened in most Catholic parishes at that time. This was back in the 1930s. They seemed much more devout than my other cousins in the ways that I had been trained to be. So why in the world would my mother seem worried about them? That's really the start of it.

By accident almost, because I was really interested in philosophy, my professor in college suggested that as far as proofs of the existence of God, [the work of] people like Maritain and Gilson on Aquinas mattered, and I got interested in Aquinas that way. So I did have an interest in Aquinas by the time I got into graduate work. Then I discovered that the Catholics were doing a lot more good scholarly work on Protestants, particularly Karl Barth, than any Protestants were doing about contemporary Catholic theological developments.

I'm afraid there was a certain amount of theological careerism operating—where was a good niche to fit in the theological scholarly spectrum? And in that regard, to become a Protestant authority on contemporary Roman Catholicism seemed like a good idea. Furthermore, as I said, I did have a certain amount of interest in Thomas Aquinas. And that's how I got started.

Studying in France in 1949

It's curious. Students, and particularly I suppose foreign students, have a tendency to be extremely parochial. I was at the École pratique des hautes études, which, like all the higher education places in France, is highly secular in terms of its government and so forth. The person I was working with chiefly was Paul Vignaux, who was a layman, a devout Roman Catholic, though that didn't show up at all in his teaching. He was dealing, with great competence, with intellectual history in the later Middle Ages. He has a little book on medieval thought that is still very readable even though it's never been translated.

My encounters with Catholics were all with lay students or teachers, and very rarely did we get around to talking about theological, contemporary developments. Then I happened to encounter some people from "Faculty Protestant," the Protestant faculty of the Reformed Church who were in dialogue with Catholic students of the Institut Catholique. In those days it was mandatory, as far as the Catholics were concerned, that Protestant students of theology here first encounter ecumenical discussions with Catholic students of theology, which was spawned, no doubt, by encounters that some of them had had during the Resistance.

In all my time in France, I didn't ever meet anybody who had had anything to do with the Vichy regime. I think that that was not only something they said, but was in fact true in my particular case. It was active Catholic students who were very much on the avant-garde, which meant that they were in favor of worker priests and so on. The *nouvelle théologie* was also of interest to them.

This was the first time that I really got involved in an ecumenical dimension anywhere in the world. I knew lots of Catholics in this country because of the work that I had been doing on the Middle Ages—but they had all been scholars and none of them dreamed, nor did I dream, of any ecumenical theological dialogue. It had been purely a matter of scholarly interest in Roman Catholic developments.

And this encounter at the Institut Catholique [that] a faculty mentor made mandatory was with Jean Daniélou. The particular first session that I went to was very memorable in my eyes. The discussion was on the Virgin Mary. It was 1950 and the dogma of the Assumption had just been proclaimed, which had horrified all Protestants. It was turning the Trinity into Quad-Trinity as far as they were concerned. We Protestants pressed very hard on this point. Notions of politeness which would prevail in a similar discussion in this country simply were absent in France! The Protestants were very vehement and rather nasty. And Daniélou was very much on the defensive. He kept on trying to explain to them that from his early childhood, asking Mary to pray for him was much more like asking his own mother to pray for him than [it was like] prayers directed to God or to Jesus. Mary was very much on the side of creatures, not God. That was my introduction to dialogue. I had not been in the least interested in ecumenism until then. I was twenty-six years old.

On the *Nouvelle Théologie*

I found out these people were interested in the visible unity of the church and were thinking and inspired in large part by the Protestant ecumenical movement, and they thought the Catholics should be part of it. The goal was the visible unity of the church. I had never encountered anybody who had ever thought that was imaginable, no matter how dismal the future.

But the people that I was talking to were students, mostly. I never encountered a professional theologian except for Jean Daniélou. Now I began reading Congar, though I had not met him. His books were never banned in any sense; his publications were not condemned. He was under severe pressure and criticism at that time, but his *Chrétiens Désunis* [*Divided Christendom*][4] was easily available. From my point of view it is in many ways the best book on Catholic ecumenism that has ever been written. It is out of date, of course, in many ways, but he strikes me as perhaps the greatest Roman Catholic ecumenist that we have.

It was the students with similar interests with whom I interacted. The person that I got to know best happened to be the head of the Roman Catholic Society at the Sorbonne at the University of Paris. I went on a pilgrimage with him and his group to Italy on the last Easter that I was there, in 1951. I was the only non-Catholic in a pilgrimage of two thousand Catholic students.

All those who were theologically interested in this pilgrimage were very much on the *nouvelle théologie* side. I must say that, like enthusiastic students most places, they were remarkably naïve. For one thing, they didn't anywhere know about the kinds of pressures that people like Congar, de Lubac, and Daniélou were under. These are things we know about now. And these students were quite willing to disregard *Humani Generis* and similar statements from the pope. They did get angry about the approaching condemnation, which had not yet occurred, of the worker priests.

And then, I remember the reception in the Vatican. We two thousand pilgrims had a so-called private audience with the pope. It was in St. Peter's. These rather seemingly anticurial students were rather Voltairean in their piety. I remember their reactions to some examples of peasant piety that we saw. I thought them utterly disgraceful with the nasty things they would say about peasant women kissing the images and so on

4. Yves Congar, *Divided Christendom* (London: Geoffrey Bles, 1939).

and so forth. After seeing some peasant women kissing St. Clare, who is in a glass enclosure in Assisi, and as we walked out the door, one of them said "La vache noire," that is, "the black cow." (The mummy is now black.) I thought it was absolutely terrible how Voltairean they were about that popular piety.

Then, at our private audience, the pope was borne in on the shoulders of the workers, and I must say that he looked rather saintly. He had a nice smile and he looked humble, which is hard to do under the circumstances. The pilgrims burst into the most enormous applause, all of them. It was like a parade of intense nationalism when the flag goes by. That made a permanent impression on me in terms of what Catholicism is like. A Catholicism of the people, a united people of many races—at least those who were really devout Catholic, and the ones I knew were devout Catholics. This is their chief nationality. This has become a kind of permanent prism through which I have seen Roman Catholicism since then.

The First Position in the Department of Philosophy at Yale University

Yale wanted to have somebody teaching medieval philosophy. And I had a dissertation on Duns Scotus, or I was writing one when I actually first began. And I knew something about Thomas Aquinas and had studied with Gilson and Vignaux. I was also teaching one-third time at the Divinity School. After ten years, it seemed to me quite clear that I didn't want to be bifurcated, and theology was my chief concern, so I just left the Philosophy Department.

Fifteen Months in Tübingen in 1959–1960

The call for the Vatican Council occurred while we were there.[5] It was a kind of crucial turning point, because I had written a

5. Professor Lindbeck received a Morse Research Fellowship from Yale to study in Tübingen in 1959.

couple of articles and I met someone who was a leader of the Roman Catholic/Lutheran ecumenical relations on the Lutheran side. He was a person who was interested in Roman Catholicism and had been interested in me for many years, indeed, as early as 1947. It would have been twelve years before I was there. He had mentioned me in a letter to Congar (which I have seen since).

Congar had become the leader of a committee that had been set up by the Lutheran World Federation for cultivating relations with Roman Catholicism. There had been theological discussions going on for many years after the end of the war in Germany in Paderborn, under the auspices of the Catholic Church and Lutheran Bishop Kristen Skydsgaard of the Lutheran World Federation, [who] was the key person. He had heard about me in North America. So in a preparatory session right after the calling of the Second Vatican Council, Skydsgaard drew together a group of people, of whom I was the one North American, to talk about what should be done to get the Lutherans ready for the council.

There was already talk about inviting the observers, but Skydsgaard decided after this meeting that a book should be written, which was to be called, I think, "The Papal Council and the Gospel." I was asked to contribute to that and write one of the articles about current developments in Roman Catholic theology. It was really that which provided the basis then for my being invited to be one of the observers to the Second Vatican Council. I think the way it happened was Skydsgaard persuaded the head of the Lutheran Church in America, Franklin Clark Frye, who was as prominent internationally as any Protestant at the time. I think that Skydsgaard got him to suggest me, but they explained to the Lutherans . . . that they needed someone who would be there regularly, and so they decided that I would also be the head of an institute that Skydsgaard had founded. I was supposed to be his successor, so to speak. So we—me and my family—were there in Rome for nearly three years, available during the council and even between sessions.

As a matter of fact, my contacts with Roman Catholics were minimal while I was in Germany. It was Lutheran ecumenism that I got involved with because I had not been involved in that at all before, and [it was] the first time I began becoming interested in ecumenism in general (to that time my focus had all been on Roman Catholicism).

These were, as you know, not mass movements. These were minority movements that felt that they were an avant-garde, but there wasn't much of a crowd behind them. Both Lutherans and the people who were on the Roman Catholic side, the people who were part of this, the leaders, the established people—professors, etc.—were under great pressures in Europe and under constant criticism that really was brutal on the Catholic side. It began changing only with the Second Vatican Council.

At Vatican II

I don't remember much from the opening service. The pattern became so familiar that it is very hard to distinguish the first from the others. After all, I was not unaccustomed to either St. Peter's or Roman Catholic masses, having been the only Protestant in a pilgrimage of two thousand!

What I do remember from the first event was afterward being questioned by a reporter from a midwestern U.S. newspaper. She had heard reports that there were Protestant observers who had knelt when the pope passed and/or greeted them. So she asked me who had knelt. I said that was obviously not my business to report, but then she asked me if I had knelt. I had not, but I realized that if she asked the question to everybody, she would be able to find out by process of elimination who had not done it. So I refused to answer the question. I could just imagine the headlines in the Midwest, some newspaper saying: "Lutheran Observer Refuses to Tell Whether He Knelt to the Pope."

The observers had weekly meetings with the Secretary of Promotion of Christian Unity. Cardinal Augustin Bea was the president of the secretariat, but the acting head at the time was Bishop Johannes Willebrands. I got to know him, as the other observers did too, quite well. My family and I lived in a very modest apartment. We invited Bishop Willebrands on one occasion to be our solo guest for an evening meal and had an absolutely charming and delightful time. He asked if it was alright to smoke a cigar at the end of the meal. My wife joined him. She liked Dutch cigars; she learned to like them from a student at Yale Divinity School. I later thought when he became a papabile or somebody who was thought of as a possible future pope, if we'd only had a picture!

I can multiply many contacts like that, with all sorts of bishops and theologians and so forth. Another, for example, was Gustave Weigel, a Jesuit—the older generation would recognize his name. He was really the leader in many respects of Catholic ecumenism before the council in this country. I'd gotten to know him and we became quite close. I felt very close, but he had so many close friends that I don't know how close he felt to me!

Oh . . . I could go on and tell so many stories. I remember one bishop of San Francisco. I will not tell his name because I cannot remember. This particular bishop got into a conversation with me at a reception at the American Embassy. We would be invited to the most extravagant, exalted kinds of receptions, all the observers. Somehow we were diplomats, not only in the eyes of the Roman Catholics but in the eyes of the world. We got into a conversation, and he'd been doing as many of the bishops were, attending the sessions of the background information that they organized by the *periti*, the Catholic advisors that the bishops had brought along. And there was one particular Catholic Scripture scholar with whom the bishop had been impressed. He wondered what we had heard and [if] we [thought] that the Scripture scholar would be a good person to bring in to give a spiritual retreat for his priests. So here was an eminent Catholic bishop who was asking a young Protestant observer for advice on what he should do for his priests.

You know, that kind of thing took place all the time. A Connecticut bishop and I had lunch together once. And he was talking to me about his thoughts [on] what Hans Küng had written about the future of the council. These were in the days when Hans Küng was, from my point of view, on the right track. I will not explain what I mean by that! He said you know the kind of things that Hans Küng wants in the council have been given a green light by the council. "I've been trained in the old school. They will remain this way until my death, you know, while remaining a bishop. I'll let things stay as much as possible as the way they were in the past. But that's the future." And the bishops knew it. Not that he voted against the Vatican II documents, but it was so alien to him that he would do nothing to promote it.

From John XXIII to Paul VI

Our perspectives are always kind of parochial. Professor Skydsgaard was the head of the three-member Lutheran World Federation contingent, and was the oldest and most experienced. He was a superb person as well as a good, even excellent theologian. Skydsgaard was a good friend of Paul VI. He had known him as Giovanni Montini before the council, when Montini was archbishop of Milan. He had a number of private sessions with him during the council, which were simply a matter of carrying on the old friendship. He had a very high esteem for Paul VI. He had the kind of personality which made him feel very sympathetic to Paul VI. He used to tell us about how terribly hard, difficult, what a cross it is to be a pope. You see, he knew of Paul VI's difficulties and how wonderfully he was rising to meet them, from Skydsgaard's point of view. I had all the sympathy in the world for Paul VI, and he was so much better a theologian than John XXIII that, by and large, I think we felt much better about the transition from John XXIII to Paul VI.

We didn't worry about John XXIII at all. John XXIII was somebody that one learned to trust very, very quickly, even when we knew that his theology was utterly primitive.

I still remember most vividly the session John XXIII had with the observers. He spoke in French, and I was very glad that I was able to understand him because it was an absolutely marvelous little off-the-cuff homily. He was talking about, you know, "I've been the kind of person who never knew what I should be doing when I woke up in the morning. It started very early. But at first it was no problem because my parents would tell me what to do. Later on in school there was no problem because my teachers would tell me what to do. And then when I became a priest, my bishop and senior pastors would sort of tell me what to do. And then when I became an archbishop of Vienna and a Cardinal, I still had people who would tell me what to do. And then I became pope!" He said, "A verse that has been very dear to me from very early in life is a verse from Lamentations about the Lord's mercies being fresh, new every morning." At this point in his recital he paused, and he said with a great smile, "And you know, it still was true, the Lord's mercies were fresh every morning." Even after he'd become pope!

John XXIII was somebody whose theological notions were utterly and completely Tridentine, but who was humble and who trusted the Spirit and who knew that a council was necessary. The pope obviously didn't interfere with the council at all. The one thing that was passed in that first session was the Constitution on the Liturgy. It was so utterly different from anything John XXIII had expected—so we assumed, because nobody said "utterly different from anything he had expected," but that was the way the Spirit was leading. That was the impression the pope gave to us.

Then came Paul VI. Paul VI had the greater mind. We were unhappy about the interventions that were being introduced by him and particularly into the Constitution of the Church. That was the major papal interference with the council. But we knew enough about such things particularly because Skydsgaard really knew about the inside workings of things. We knew that he judged that it was politically necessary in terms of intrachurch politics. We were willing to take Skydsgaard's word that Paul VI was probably right about all of that, that it was necessary. And, by the way, that intervention did horrify the observers in general. But because of the Skydsgaard connection, Lutherans weren't as horrified as others.

On Albert Outler and Other Observers
from the United States

I was a former student of Albert Outler's. I had a course from him at Yale Divinity School while he was teaching there, before he went to Perkins. We knew each other. We were friendly. We were not close at all. We never became close. During the council, he was the chief person on the American side. The Americans would gather independently of their denominational connections except for a few people, Lutherans like myself. My job, however, was not to stay in touch with the Americans but with Lutherans, and the Lutheran bishops that I was supposed to stay in touch with were the French-speaking ones, which in those days actually meant something. It included all the Spanish ones because almost all of the Lutheran bishops from Latin America could speak French well in those days. So that was my job. French and Latin American Lutheran bishops—I had very little to do with the Americans [at the council].

After the Council

Because of my spirit at the council, I was the person who wrote the initial memoranda about starting the Lutheran/Roman Catholic dialogue, both in United States and internationally. I was involved in starting the dialogues from the very beginning, especially the American, and then later on, as the American dialogue developed, the international dialogue. The international dialogue, of course, was the major contact with Roman Catholic theologians, although one of them had started earlier because I had been a teaching assistant to John Courtney Murray.

John Courtney Murray was in many ways the best known Catholic theologian at the time, and he was part of the initial U.S. dialogue. I had been teaching assistant to him back in 1952 at Yale when he was brought in as the first Roman Catholic priest ever to teach at Yale, and then he went into the Philosophy Department. They asked him to teach medieval philosophy, which he didn't know anything about, really! He felt compelled to do something about the Greek background for a lecture on medieval philosophy. He gave a lecture on Plato and Aristotle, and the majors in the class found the lectures utterly hopeless—as they should have! So, as teaching assistant, along with another person, we got together with Murray and told him, really, why this was very bad. He responded magnificently. He gave a lecture of retraction and spent a half hour talking about what he should have said and not said. Knowing firsthand the spirit of the most prominent Roman Catholic theologian in the country and then the other Roman Catholics, I eagerly engaged in the Lutheran/Roman Catholic dialogue.

Shifts from the Late 1960s to the 1970s

This is oversimplifying, as everything here is oversimplified. But I read Victor Preller's *Divine Science and the Science of God* in 1967. It was two years before it was published. I was asked to read it by the publishers to see whether it was worthy of publication. I thought it was magnificent. It opened my eyes to a way of reading Aquinas that I had not yet seen. But Preller really should have said something about what is called transcendental Thomism—which includes [Karl] Rahner (and Lonergan, though not anywhere near as genuinely as in the case of Rahner). So I wrote in the report to the publisher that Preller really had to mention transcendental Thomism in order to satisfy people who would expect it. Preller made the changes. He never knew that it was I who suggested them. He made the changes, and then two years later the book was published. I think my part in it is probably my greatest contribution to scholarship.

If you use catchwords, an analytic, philosophical reading of Aquinas made sense, and that made me very skeptical of transcendental Thomism. I began seeing all sorts of problems with Rahner that I had not seen before. But it wasn't until 1973 that I began reading David Burrell. Of course, it was his second book (*Aquinas: God and Action*), not the first (*Analogy and Philosophical Language*), that had the most influence on me. In the 1970s there was this development of understanding doctrine as this linguistic exercise and practice that called into question the anchoring of theology in a kind of a transcendental subjectivity.

I don't know how to bridge the gap logically from the analytic reading of Thomas to ecumenism, but the great problem of the ecumenical dialogues became a problem that anyone who has happened to have looked at *The Nature of Doctrine* will be aware of, namely, the problem that I call the matter of "reconciliation without capitulation." That is to say, one hears this phrase in these dialogues over and over again. Let me take a relatively logically simple case: the relationships between the Lutheran and Roman Catholic teachings on the Eucharist. The "real presence" is the traditional Lutheran phrase, [meaning that] Christ's body is truly present, in, with, and under the elements of the Eucharist, in contrast to what I hope is a not unfamiliar phrase, transubstantiation, [in which] the elements change into the body and the blood of Christ even though the appearances remain bread and wine.

It did not take very long before both sides agreed that this was not to be understood as doctrinally divisive. Transubstantiation depended upon a particular perspective, an Aristotelian metaphysical perspective, and it was the Aristotelian way of saying that Christ's body and blood is truly present in the Lord's Supper . . . even the elements, while their chemical composition and so on remains the same. These are two different ways of affirming the same truth.

Here I am going to make a slight change. I am going to introduce a slight deviation. The real problem in Eucharistic discussions was the sacrifice of the mass. The dispute there is the offering of Christ in the Eucharist and a second offering in addition to the sacrifice on the cross, adding something to the sacrifice of Christ on the cross. Of course the Protestants, starting with the Lutherans, said firmly "No," which is why we do not call the Eucharist a sacrifice except as a sacrifice of thanksgiving.

The discussions ended up being over a matter of practice: the so-called multiplication of the masses—the more masses the better. Only because the council said, "No, the ideal way of celebrating is a communal celebration, and to have many celebrations instead of one communal celebration is worse rather than better." That, of course, settled it. It was a practical issue—it ended up being a matter of practice that determined whether there was a community division at this point.

The philosophical/analytic approach, with the help of Wittgenstein and Thomas Aquinas (very much in terms of his practice, his way of reconciling all sorts of people who apparently disagreed with him), was the answer of how to deal with this question of how there could be reconciliation without capitulation. But it involves practice, language, and conceptual analysis—all three.

Through developing new conceptual tools, one could try to retrieve what was really at stake in an issue. I mean to say that it seems to me that in many ways (I don't know that any of the patristics scholars would agree with this) if you want to find out what the fathers thought as a group, read Thomas. I mean that is obviously oversimplified. He didn't have a grasp of the practice and so forth. But Thomas can be used to return to an early Christian center.

On *The Nature of Doctrine*

It has been hard for people to accept that *The Nature of Doctrine* is about intra-Christian theological and ecumenical issues. I suppose it is because I state its ecumenical purpose in the introduction and then do not keep on saying it throughout. The things that are not directly related to the doctrinal question of how one understands doctrine are simply secondary. I try to say that in the book but manage it very poorly. I was addressing the book to a very much more restricted audience. I thought I was going to be read by ecumenists who were also well-trained theologians. I was trying to explain how this kind of theological task was compatible with all sorts of other views, including some thoroughly modern ones, including the cultural linguistic view, for example, of anthropologists such as Clifford Geertz.

It is hard for me to explain, because the book taught me a good lesson that many, many authors have, I think, experienced. A book gets out there and is read in many different ways. It is written about in many different ways, and you read the criticisms and you re-read the book again and say, "Yes, I can see how it can be interpreted that way." And after awhile it ceases to be your own work. It's kind of like a Rorschach that's out there. You read all sorts of pictures into this Rorschach book and in many ways that is how I find myself reacting to the book now. I find myself saying, "Yes, I see [what I should have done] in order to avoid (from the terms of my initial intentions) those misunderstandings." When I look at it that way, the book is an utter mess!

I think I was thinking habitus every time I wrote about people like Geertz and so on. I was trying to make it appealing. Let me try to explain it in a little more simplified manner: the major structural problem in the book, which I myself mention in the book, is that I borrow a lot of modern terminology and conceptuality that fit in with what I was trying to say because, after all, I wanted to speak to as wide an audience as I could. But I had width; I did not have quantity in mind. I didn't really expect it to sell so well—and it still keeps on selling, you see.

At the same time, I talk about how Christian theology must not be built on foundations other than biblical foundations. To use the expression I used, the biblical world should absorb the world, rather than be founded on nonbiblical, intellectual views. I contradict myself, in a way. That is the major problem with the book. But I recognize that and I say it at the end.

Joint Lutheran/Roman Catholic Statement on Justification

The Joint Declaration is a product of the ecumenical conversations that have been going on in the national/international level for thirty-odd years, since the '60s. It was issued in 1999. That was thirty-two years since the beginning of the formal conversations on the international level. And, you know, I was involved in these discussions to some extent, but I cannot say that I made any more of a contribution or made as much of a contribution as several other people. It is an example, very much, of what I referred to before as "reconciliation without capitulation."

The procedure is in many ways influenced by the medieval and the Thomas Aquinas question approach. You raise a question, and then there is an objection to the position that you're going to take, and then you try to answer the objection. I would say that what I'm trying to do in *The Nature of Doctrine*—[to develop] a so-called rule theory of doctrine, a grammatical rule theory of doctrine—is an attempt then to provide a supporting conceptuality for seeing how this "question method" proceeds and how apparently contradictory views can be shown not to contradict each other [if one illustrates] the appropriate distinctions.

The original Reformation demand as articulated by the Augsburg Confession in 1530 was that the freedom of the gospel be granted, and that meant the freedom to preach justification by faith in Jesus Christ alone. The location of the "alone" in that statement is important. It's not faith alone; it's Jesus Christ alone. God as known in Jesus Christ is what one has faith in.

Now from the point of view of the declaration, that freedom to proclaim justification by faith has now been granted by Roman Catholics. This means that from the point of the Reformation, its origins, the one reason for not submitting to Rome—so to speak, in not acknowledging the bishop of Rome as a legitimate minister of the church universal—has been granted. This raises the question, "Why not reunite?" And I think almost all of the divisive issues that now remain have arisen since the Reformation.

From the point of view of a Lutheran who takes the declaration seriously, Lutherans have to explain why they have difficulties in reuniting with Rome. As I put in an autobiographical piece that I wrote recently, Lutherans are the only people left in the world who still really can talk about what is needed, [which] is [a] return to Rome. Rome doesn't talk that way anymore, but in terms of the beginnings and first causes of the Reformation, we now have to explain why we can't return to Rome. We Lutherans pictured ourselves as a reform movement within the Catholic Church of the West. That is very much the way that the Augsburg Confession is written. We claim that everything we said was in conformity with Roman doctrine as taught by the early fathers. (The early fathers that the declaration mentions are Ambrose and Augustine.)

Now, I am the only Lutheran who ever talks that way. No, wait, I shouldn't put it that way. There are lots of Catholic Lutherans who talk the way I have—but the particular phrase of "return to Rome" is one that only I am comfortable with.

His Work as Preparation for the Future

The one advantage of living a long time is that one mistrusts entirely predictions of what the future will bring. And if you suppose that present trends will still be the major trends ten years from now, you have a better than fifty/fifty chance that you will be mistaken. So consider any of my comments on the future in that light.

What is the future of ecumenism? I grew up at a time when a sense of ecumenism and an interest in the visible unity of the church were collapsing. That is to say, my earliest memories of ecumenism were back from the 1930s, when I was a teenager. At that time, what was happening in the so-called ecumenical movement was the predominance of what was called work and life. The social agenda of the Christian church had taken predominance over faith and order, which was concerned with unity of the divided fragments of Christ's body. The missionary groups that I was growing up amid, not only the Lutherans but others too, weren't the least interested in an ecumenicity of faith and order. The major voice in ecumenism at that time was the book called *The Laymen's Report on the Missionary Movement*, which sounds very much like anti-ecumenical concern for social action and for the unity of religions rather than intra-Christian unity.

But then look what happened. It started really with the First World War but didn't touch Americans until the Second World War, in the so-called neo-orthodox movement. The neo-orthodox movement reinvigorated interest in intra-Christian unity grounded in a historic Christianity. I'm speaking particularly about Barth, but then you have to include not only people like Brunner, but also Tillich as well. Read now, you don't see why you'd call Tillich neo-orthodox at all—that's because of what has been done with Tillich. Tillich can be read two different ways. He is one of the most ambiguous writers that I know. But he can be read as an orthodox Christian from the point of view of historic Christianity, and he also can be read as a flaming liberal of a certain kind. At any rate, neo-orthodoxy transforms the ecumenical movement too. And if you think that this century will be any more spared the kinds of depths of despair as represented by the Second World War, you are likely to be mistaken. I mean, we now have not only political problems like Communism and Nazism, but we are destroying the world with environmental problems and economic collapse in this country, a collapse which may eventually make the depression period look minor. If we escape that for a century, then I am altogether wrong.

At any rate, given the revolutions that are likely to be taken and the way we find ourselves reacting to reality, I can't help but think that there is at least a good chance that the sorts of things that drove the church to what we call neo-orthodoxy[6] that required a realizable interest in the visible unity of the churches, is something we won't escape in this century either. That's the way I look at the future. Therefore I think of what I have been doing all my life in working for the visible unity of the church,

6. Professor Lindbeck here seems to refer to the conflagrations of World Wars I and II and the tensions and violence of Cold War.

even though now the interest in it is minimal in comparison to what it was forty years ago . . . [and] I cannot help but think of it except as preparation for something that in all likelihood, even by nontheological, purely worldly considerations, might very well be very valuable in the things that will be happening in the not very distant future.

So I am quite willing to leave this life, and quite optimistic about my life's work.

4

"In the Beginning, God Created the Heavens and the Earth"

An Interview with David Burrell

*Father David Burrell's life is unintelligible without a particu-
lar place called the University of Notre Dame (Notre Dame,
Indiana) and the community of nuns and priests called the
Congregation of the Holy Cross. Father Burrell arrived at
Notre Dame's golden dome as a teenager, and he has lived and
worked throughout the world in places such as Jerusalem, Palestine; Cairo, Egypt; Dhaka, Bangladesh; Durham, England;
Princeton, New Jersey; and Nkozi, Uganda. Given the finest
philosophical education in analytic philosophy possible in his
day at Yale University, Father Burrell found himself retooling
in "mid-career" in Cairo to learn Arabic in order to read medieval Islamic thought in its own language. The resultant breadth
of his witness has ranged across four continents. His life and
work highlight the very concrete nature of the catholicity of the*

church across space; his engagement with Aquinas as a contemporary source for intra-Abrahamic faith dialogues witnesses to the concreteness of the same catholicity of the church across time. The Catholic Theological Society of America recognized the significance of Father Burrell's lifetime of theological work by awarding him the John Courtney Murray Award, its highest award, in 2009.

Childhood Background

My father came from Scottish Presbyterian background. My mother's grandfather had been a Congregational minister in upstate New York who had converted to Catholicism during the Oxford Movement in the middle of the nineteenth century. There are just incredible connections from growing up in an ecumenical household. I once asked my father why he didn't come to church with us. He said, "Well, you know, I went to church with your mother when we were first married, and every time I went they preached against mixed marriages!" That was my dad's ticket out.

The important thing was that he was a great cook and my mother was not. We had four boys and a girl in the family. My mother said, "There is not girl's work and boy's work; there is just work!" So my father directed us to the kitchen. My father would stay home and cook this wonderful brunch for us [that we ate] when we got home from Mass every Sunday morning, and that became the place where we would bring friends. As we grew up, if we were interested in someone, we would bring her to Sunday brunch. So we had a way by which we continued our Eucharist around Sunday brunch. It was a very important thing.

Shortly after John F. Kennedy was shot, my dad had a serious bleeding ulcer; all four of his sons came to see him in the hospital. I had been ordained a priest for about three years, and I thought maybe "Gee, you know, if Dad is going to die, I better say something to him." So I tried to say something to my father. What do you say pastorally to your father? He said,

"I've always tried to treat people the way Jesus would. That is what my mother taught me." So I backed out of the room—and that was the end of that.

The other point I want to make is that George's answers to the questions and his response to the avenues that Providence opened up in his life remind me of a wonderful proverb, "Events blindside us all." It is very important that the call of Providence be answered in the events of our lives.

Education in Rome

I arrived in Rome in 1956, to study at the Gregorian. We went through the death of Pius XII and the accession of John XXIII, previously Angelo Roncalli, the Patriarch of Venice, to the papacy. The first thing I realized in Rome was how Protestant I was when I got there. As an American Catholic, you realize how Protestant you are. It is reflected in all sorts of ways. In the American Catholic community if someone becomes a priest, it is really an honor. In Italy, the young women say, "What a waste!" So I learned that anticlericalism is a part of a Catholic diet.

I studied under Bernard Lonergan. Lonergan was an eastern Canadian. During the time that I went there, all the teachers still taught in Latin. But they really didn't teach in Latin; for the Germans you had to wait until the end of the sentence for the verb. They taught in their own language with a kind of Latin. And I think Lonergan was understood by all the Anglo-Saxons, but the Latins couldn't figure Lonergan out at all!

The beauty of Lonergan was that he showed the importance of intellectual and particularly philosophical elaboration in theology, yet [put it in] its proper place. The way he did this was following. He used to divide the world—which has helped me continuously all the way through my life—between those who need certitude and those who search for understanding.

Somebody said, "Yeah, you search for certainty." . . . No! Different verbs! "Needing" certitude requires a psychological verb. If you look back at Descartes's *Discourse on Method*, you realize it is a psychological treatise. He is trying to find something certain to hold onto psychologically. Many Christians do that with doctrine. "Whereas," Lonergan said, "doctrine is rather the search for understanding." He had the quickest and simplest explanation of hermeneutics, which the Germans could never help me understand. He said, "If Chalcedon is given to us as a set of answers, then what we have to do is understand what the questions were to which those were the answers." If we do theology in that way, then we'll understand how it is that we are to do it ourselves but in fidelity to the way in which the early church traced the doctrine of Jesus, the ontological constitution of Jesus as the Christ.

So what I learned from Lonergan was how to look at the great theologians of the world as asking questions rather than giving answers. As I followed the questions and the structure of the *Summa Theologiae* of Thomas, I would learn how to do theology from the questions. Doing theology became a mode of apprenticeship under the masters.

Do you know Thomas Merton's wonderful Zen story about the apprentice and the master butcher, in which the apprentice feels like he is oppressed? The apprentice said to the master, "Look, you've had the same cleaver all the time I've been an apprentice to you. You earn much more than I do. I've had to buy a new cleaver every three months!" The master says, "I've been waiting for you to ask that question. Why do you think you have to buy a new cleaver every three months?" The apprentice replies, "It gets dull." The master says, "It's because you haven't watched me. When that cleaver finds the appropriate space, it goes right through." So that's what masters teach you.

The Intellectual Climate in Rome

Nouvelle théologie was the name of the game when I was studying in Rome. The same kind of *nouvelle théologie* that George met in France had even penetrated to the academic and intellectual circles in Rome. All of the theologians that we had in

Rome were attuned to it; their mode was very deductive—but you could work through that. Our Scripture people at the Gregorian were terrible. They were doing excellent Scripture studies across the street at the Pontifical Biblical Institute. We had a French library in our house, and so we read de Lubac and those people and got our own Scripture education.

Graduate Education after Rome

My post-Rome graduate education had to do with cultural things, about Catholics and Protestants in the early 1960s, which I think is important for people to understand. I belong to a religious congregation of men and women, priests, brothers, and sisters founded 175 years ago by a French curé who had the radical view of a religious congregation that was a microcosm of the church—male and female, lay and clerical. He even masked that radicality from himself with the pious image of the holy family. It was very important that members of that religious congregation get higher degrees in order to allow Notre Dame to progress as a true university. By the time that I returned to Notre Dame, Father Ted Hesburgh was president. He had great ambitions for the university. Those of us who were inclined to study in various fields were very crucial to that goal. By the grace of God, I had an older colleague by the name of Ernan McMullen, who was an Irish priest. He had a degree in physics and in philosophy from Dublin and from Louvain. Ernan said to me, "Look, Catholic religious congregations always send their people to Europe to do philosophy." He had just finished an NEH Fellowship at Yale, and he said, "Graduate study is as much networking as it is learning, and so you should do your graduate studies here in the U.S. if Notre Dame wants to become a university in an American sense. Yale is probably the best place."

I had difficulty negotiating that with my religious congregation. Our director of studies was a man who had done his doctoral work at Labelle in Quebec, and Labelle had a much more hidebound, neo-Thomist view of the world than I had learned from Lonergan. We compromised. He said, "I think you should spend a year at Labelle and study the texts of St. Thomas, and then you can go wherever you want to study." This is kind of the way obedience was beginning to work in religious congregations after Vatican II.

It was the best thing I ever did—I got a couple of articles from that year published. It was all in French. I really improved my French. I was sitting on the banks of the St. Lawrence, cooling my heels in January, and I was accepted at Yale and Princeton. I am so happy I went to Yale. I did not want to go to Princeton because Walter Kauffman, who was very antireligious, was there, and I didn't want to have to fight that too. I found a wonderful environment at Yale, a very receptive environment. I had great students. I did not even go near the Divinity School, because I wanted to learn logic and analytic philosophy. That's what I really wanted to do. I just was turning thirty, and nobody could be trusted after thirty back in the '60s, so I wanted to get finished quickly with my graduate studies.

From Rome to Yale

I had grown up in a family that was ecumenical. With others, I was ordained into the priesthood at the end of 1959, in Rome. They ordained us because they wanted help in the parishes in Rome during Advent, for confessions. The reason they wanted help in the parishes in Rome during Advent is because there is a priest shortage in Rome (in case you don't know that). And so, in my very first confession, I am out there very exposed and kind of putting up a bunch of confessionals around, and a man comes up to me—this is the only confession I have ever been able to tell! So he tells me, in a typically Italian way, "Father, I did a little bit of everything!" That was my pastoral introduction to Italy.

I was not in Rome during the Second Vatican Council. I did have wonderful friends there. We were just excited about what was going on, and it was liturgically and theologically very important. As the council began, we felt that we were in a very privileged position because the theology we had learned was essentially the theology that was being disseminated by the council. We were kind of on the crest of a wave. Pastorally, we were very much in favor of the liturgical renewal of the church. We felt we had a marvelous way of moving together to open up Catholicism to the wider world.

My time at the More House at Yale was very important to me. There were two Roman Catholic priests there—a Jesuit who was a Republican and me, who was Holy Cross. We were not a model of the community! In my second year, I got a Danforth Fellowship, a Camp Fellowship. I was living with our Holy Cross brothers in New Haven, which is what we often do in graduate school. Somebody else was going to take my room, so I had a little money to pay More House, the Catholic chaplaincy at Yale. It was constructed by the personal funds of a man named T. Lorrison Riggs, who was an Episcopal convert to Catholicism, from the Riggs National Bank family in Washington. More House was an elegant place and a good community. I served as a priest there. That's where we did a lot of learning together—pastoral response, for example, to *Humanae Vitae* and the whole issue of contraception. We would talk about that so that in confessional policy, we would have a common policy—the three of us there would embrace it. It was a wonderful learning experience.

John Kennedy was killed when I was at Yale. We all remember, of our generation, where we were when that happened. I was actually in the locker room after a game of squash. We went right over to More House. Jim Healy was the chaplain. I said, "What are we going to do?" He said, "We'll call Bill Coffin." William Sloane Coffin was the chaplain at Yale. I called up Bill, and I said, "Bill, what should we do?" He said, "God damn it, have Mass!" So, we functioned in a deeply ecumenical environment there.

The *Humanae Vitae* question, which came up in 1968, was the pastoral "clinch" for us Catholics and particularly for priests. I had a very good friend named Sebastian Moore who was then serving as a parish priest in Liverpool. He was a monk; he used to send out this mimeographed stuff about how we were to respond to the encyclical, thinking it through as priests, and leading people. It was what we discussed at the dinner table at Yale. So we were a part of the pastoral/theological inquiry that was going on very vigorously.

Back to Notre Dame

A Jesuit can make a transcendental argument that teaching Ugaritic is his pastoral work. As Holy Cross priests, we can't do that. We live with the students. This is one of the things that makes Notre Dame very special. We do not turn the student living situations/residence halls over to the youth culture for two reasons. One is we know who is paying the bills, and second, we know that there are a lot of unscrupulous adults making a lot of money on the youth culture. So it's not exactly a tight ship, but we do have single-sex residence halls, and you can argue that interminably but, again, we know who pays the bills.

I returned to Notre Dame in 1964 and kind of hunkered down to finish my dissertation. I was living with young men in residence halls, and that means that I was involved in the wee hours of the morning. Your whole life got turned around after they got back from the library with the kinds of decisions they were forced to make vis-à-vis Vietnam. In 1965 I was open to these things. It was a terribly important time for thinking through issues about just war, selective service/conscientious objection, and all that business. One of the fringe benefits we had was that we had a ritual. We didn't have to invent one. There was a lot of inventing of rituals going on in the '60s. During the moratorium in the fall of 1969, we had a liturgy on the main quad in front of the library in which we gathered everyone together. We had worked with five or six students for a long time because we wanted to make certain that they tore up their draft cards, each one personally. They tore up their draft cards in the middle of the liturgy. The FBI was there, of course, taking pictures. It was a way of expressing that as Christians, we simply could not be involved in this kind of a conflict. I could be involved in other kinds of conflicts. I am not as staunch a pacifist as Stanley [Hauerwas] is, I don't think. I am not sure where my position is, but at least I was strong on the just war criteria. That time was a crucible. We had to bring together theory and practice and try to help students understand what their responsibilities were as Christians.

I had to bring together my life as a priest, a philosophical theologian, and an ethicist. I was teaching logic and philosophy of science. In the fall of 1969, things heated up. In the spring of 1970 Cambodia and Kent State happened, and it really heated up. After that summer several people came back in the fall of 1970 and they were just tired—they were strung out, and so we could begin to do some work in philosophical theology. My colleagues in the Theology Department encouraged me to accept their invitation to be chair of the Theology Department. That was a wonderful step in my life. Stanley was one of those colleagues. With Lonergan's help, it was then that my work in logic and philosophy of science began to translate into philosophical theology—and that was much more germane to my whole person.

In 1971 I became chair of the Department of Theology. And so, somehow or another, the two sides of my life came together better, and I could focus on philosophical theology. For some reason, somebody that reviewed metaphysics asked me (which again is Providence) to review Victor Preller's *Divine Science and the Science of God* . . . which I did. I was very taken with it. The journal gave me three books to review, and the other two were not worth much, so I spent the time on Preller.

During this time of Vietnam and everything else, Stanley arrived. We had a wonderful discussion group in our Philosophy Department. We would meet at someone's home—I think it was a Tuesday evening—once a month. Someone decided we would read through Wittgenstein. Here you have a bunch of faculty, younger and older, grappling with the work of Wittgenstein in the way in which philosophers do. It was just an education in itself. I think we carried that on for almost a decade.

Notre Dame and the American Reception of Vatican II

Father Hesburgh had inaugurated a Center for Continuing Education with a medium we called "Vat Two-and-a-half." He brought to Notre Dame as many of the distinguished periti (the theological expert advisers of the bishops at Vatican II) as he could, and also Protestant observers like George, Catholic ones like John Courtney Murray, and even some of the bishops. Al Outler became really a very dear friend. I did a semester at SMU where I wanted to come to grips with the work of Schubert Ogden because I could not understand this process theology stuff. I came to realize that there wasn't much there to understand! I finally came to see that if you were a liberal Christian, and you had to find a place for Jesus, then you needed some philosophy to do it. But if you hung on with Chalcedon, you were okay without it. But that's another story. Shu and I agreed to disagree on most every topic, but we became good colleagues.

I always felt myself in those years as part of a current that was moving very strongly, often in different ways, but that the guidance I had from Lonergan gave me a huge start—[reminding me that I] don't need certitude but [must] seek understanding. And so I would take understanding from wherever it came.

I think that George said some very prophetic things in those days—particularly in *The Future of Roman Catholic Theology*—that are only finding their way right now, even in my life. I now live in Jerusalem with a minority of Christians in the land where Jesus lived, squeezed between two majorities—one of which still thinks of itself as a minority, but that just complicates the matter. I have come to see that maybe as Christians, the only way we can really be Christians (and I learned this from Stanley and John Howard Yoder, of course) is to understand that we need a community that nourishes friendship, [and we need] to learn how to follow Jesus because the external signs are not going to point in that direction. That was part of my postliberal move, if you will.

Friendship with Stanley Hauerwas

Stan and I wrote several articles together. We did not stick too much on "fields" and "descriptors" like ethicist and philosophical theologian. We were simply friends who were inquirers. Stanley taught me a lot. We had team-taught a course on self-deception, and that was a very important thing to me. First I learned collaboration as a goal from Lonergan. He himself was not a very good collaborator at all, but he talked about collaboration. But it was and still is very important to me that publication and teaching reinforce one another. To have publication come out of teaching was something I wanted to promote for myself and for others. I did not want the "publish or perish" attitude to dominate so that you thought your teaching was less important than your writing.

"From System to Story," in any event, was the key article Stanley and I did together. It is now quoted in bibliographies as an early article on narrative theology. This was an attempt to use the narrative mode to get at philosophical thinking in practical reason or ethics. It brought together various strands of thought that had impacted us both. We would divide the essay into parts. We would each write a part and then let the other rewrite the same part. It was simple, but a good way of working.

On a "Catholic" University

We have to recognize what the word *catholic* can do and what *catholic* can't do as the great tradition. It wasn't until I was chair of the Theology Department and began to work with the divinity school deans—Yale, Union, and Chicago were the "biggies" at the time—that I began to realize there was an ideology working there. The ideology was that theology started with Schleiermacher! The rest was the history of Christian thought. It was all treated as background, you see.

Then I realized, however, that each of these principal places had had a key person teaching the history of Christian thought: Robert Calhoun at Yale, Jaroslav Pelikan at Chicago. The history of Christian thought was part of Christian theology! It wasn't just background. That was a terribly important insight to me because I began to realize that the schools that were in the Reformation tradition had tended to think that they had started it all over again and that theology started with them—and this other stuff was, at best, background. I think that what we can do in a Catholic university is recover this historical, continuous sense of Christian theology. This is what the *ressourcement* did, and this is why Vatican II was so crucial.

Catholics had gotten caught in the same thing as Protestants, which is what Hegel talks about. When I was living with our brothers in West Haven in 1962–1963, I came across a book, a big fat book in the library published in 1907, called something like *The Fundamentals of Catholic Teaching*. And, the fundamentals of Catholic teaching were—surprise, surprise—real presence in the Eucharist, blessed Virgin Mary, and indulgences and purgatory. In other words, the "fundamentals" were the very things that had stuck like a bone in the throat of the Protestant Reformation. The Counter-Reformation, to my understanding, was as myopic as the Reformation. That is why the *ressourcement* and Vatican II were so important. It allowed us to see the tradition as continuous while simultaneously seeing that different modalities exist in the tradition. These different modalities were very important to bring out different accents in the searching for the truth, which always lies beyond us.

As Chair of the Department of Theology at Notre Dame

Father Hesburgh had been given a Judaica position for the university from a wealthy family. He gave it to the Department of Theology, as he always did. Now what are we going to do with it? If we had been a religious studies department, we could have hired some rabbi and had him off in the corner teaching rabbinics. It wouldn't have made any difference at all. I always used to commiserate with my friends who taught in secular universities where they had only religious studies—I say this as a professionally religious person. I find religion most of the time deadly boring but God most infinitely interesting. I don't want to be in a religious studies department.

We always described ourselves as a Department of Theology in a Catholic university. We described ourselves that way because we were ecumenical in spirit. We felt that the presence of these other voices would only enrich our ongoing Catholic tradition. The Judaica position was very important though, because we had to think through what we were going to do with this position. Thanks to the help of Stanley Hauerwas, Joe Blenkinsopp (Hebrew Scriptures), and Robert Wilken (early church), we said, "Hey, Robert Wilken had already done a book on Chrysostom and the Jews; Joe Blenkinsopp was working in the Second Temple Period . . . why don't we fold the Judaica position into a group which we can rename as 'Judaism and Christianity in Antiquity.'" So we put the new Judaica position at the very center of our theological endeavor, namely within our study of Scripture and early church. I think that was just a brilliant move. We were given all sorts of kudos by the external reviewers of the department. I think that was one of the best things we did.

It set me up because having spent all this time in Jewish Christian understanding, I came to realize that you cannot be a Christian without understanding yourself first as a Jew. *Nostra Aetate* had helped immensely in this regard. All of the major documents of Vatican II had already been prepared for by the *nouvelle théologie*. Two documents that came out of Vatican II were really fruits of the council. Although there had been prior preparation, theologians had done not nearly the extensive work to prepare for *Nostra Aetate*, on the relation of church with other religions, and *Dignitatis Humanae*, the document on religious freedom. Those really came out of the council itself. I was very fascinated with this relationship of Christianity and Judaism and how Judaism had really forced itself to define itself over against this Jesus movement. Nonetheless, you could not be part of the Jesus movement unless you understood that the Scriptures meant the Hebrew Scriptures.

Engaging Jewish, Christian, and Islamic Relations through Thomas Aquinas

At the end of my nine years as chair of the department, Father Hesburgh asked me if I would be rector of the Ecumenical Institute at Tantur in Jerusalem. In the meantime I had taught for a semester in Bangladesh, a 92-percent Muslim country. My heart had been attracted to Islam, though I knew nothing about it. In Jerusalem, I could encounter both Muslims and Jews. In the two years that I spent there, I began to learn Arabic with the realization that if I was going to do Jewish/Christian things, I also had to fold in Islam.

Now there was another reason for this. I am a great fan of Charles Sanders Peirce—the great American philosopher who always thought in triads. Triads are very important because bipolar relationships can get stuck. That is why we have marriage counselors! It isn't that you always have to have three people around the table, but if the Jewish-Christian thing gets stuck—and God knows it has gotten stuck over the politics of the state of Israel, which is the one thing you cannot talk about in Jewish-Christian dialogue—then it is always good to have Islam as a third point. We use the word *triangulate*—and that became very key to my theological life.

I began to look at the relationship between Judaism, Christianity, and Islam in relationship to an understanding of creation. With de Lubac I began to realize that we could not make such an absolute divide between nature and supernatural, and that [because] the nature/supernatural distinction pervaded all of life, that led you deeper into Aquinas and deeper into creation. My real argument with Schubert Ogden had been that process theology does not know what to do with creation. Creation is the first gift. Our problem in the nature/grace distinction was simply the way it was posed. If grace is a gift, what's nature? A given? Of course not; it's a gift! The more you immerse yourself in patristic thought, whenever you talk about creation, you have to talk about redemption. And whenever you talk about redemption, you have to talk about creation.

This comes out in the Muslim world by saying that once you immerse yourself in the Qur'an, then you can begin to see the world as signs of God's presence. And the very word *sign* is also the word for *verse* in the Qur'an, so that if you immerse yourself in the Qur'an you are in a position to see the world as created by God; otherwise you are not. Hans Frei was really important to me in all of this. This whole sense in which the Scriptures become the world in which you live, through which you begin to see the other world in which you live . . . there is a dialectic, in that sense, of reason and faith.

One has to learn what distinction is involved when one makes a distinction. One of the most difficult things in teaching a philosophy course is to teach students the meaning of distinction . . . that it does not mean a separation. But it does mean a distinction. And it is terribly important. We see this in human relationships. You're not separate, nor are you clumped together. You are distinct. Particularly in male/female relationships, this is a terribly important thing to understand: that you are distinct and yet together. So I think there are very practical analogs to this.

My Aquinas book was published in 1979; I had finished it earlier. On the way to Jerusalem in 1980, I stopped at Louvain. Franklin Robb, who had been one of our faculty members, had a supper in which there was a distinguished Dominican. I told him I had just finished a book on Aquinas and I would really like him to review it. He got a little smile on his face, and he said, "I just did." I didn't have the courage to ask him what he said!

When I went to Jerusalem, I had finished a book on Aquinas. Of course like any young man, at the time I thought it was the last book that needed to be written on Aquinas. But I knew nothing about his dependence on Moses Maimonides, a Jew, and Ibn-Sina, a Muslim. I knew *that* he was dependent upon them, but the irony is that almost all of the scholarship on Aquinas had been done in northern Europe. I came, however, to realize that biographically Thomas came from the Mediterranean. At the end of his life when he was asked to start a *studium* for theology in his Italian province, he did not situate it in Orvieto, which would have been up north where the papal court was, but in Naples, where he grew up. Naples was part of the kingdom of the two Siciles. They were commissioning translations there from Arabic writings. Then you look at the map, and you say, "Wow!" Europe was separated from the Middle East and North Africa by the Mediterranean, but land travel was virtually impossible. And they didn't have to get there "yesterday," so sea travel was the way they did it. Also the Crusades were going on, and one of the fringe benefits of war (the only fringe benefit perhaps) is cultural exchange.

Then I stayed in Jerusalem a second year after being Rector at Tantur before they found my successor. I began to study Moses Maimonides as a key bridge figure between the two. Moses Maimonides was a Jew, a Sephardic Jew. He had grown up in Cordova, well before 1492, so he wasn't forced out by Ferdinand and Isabella. He was forced out by rude, crude Almohads, that is, a Muslim group that came up to help the Muslims resist the Reconquista from the Christians and the northern part of the Iberian Peninsula. So his Jewish family had to leave, whereas previously the Muslim governors in Andalusia had been very tolerant of Jews and Christians as peoples of the book. He found his way to Fustat in Cairo, where he grew up in a virtually Islamic world. When Maimonides wrote *The Guide of the Perplexed*, his aim was to show young, believing Jews how they could study philosophy not only without losing their faith but in order to deepen their faith. What was Aquinas's goal with Aristotle? Exactly the same goal! To show believing Christians that they could adopt this philosophy (they would have to transform it in the process) not only without losing their faith but to deepen their faith.

So Aquinas read *The Guide of the Perplexed* as soon as it got into Latin. I have shown how on five key issues Aquinas is beholden to Maimonides. So you have an interior kind of relationship between a Jewish and a Christian thinker. They couldn't meet each other because their life spans were fifty years separate. But you and I well know that when we read a person we are dialoguing with them, and that is what Aquinas was doing with Maimonides. Maimonides imbibed Islamic thought, and then he also got translations of Ibn-Sina, who gave him a very key distinction for formulating his understanding of creation. So I began to see—my heavens!—[that] what most people recognize as the classic synthesis of Christian theology was already an interfaith, intercultural achievement. So that is what we should be doing in our time. That's my understanding.

From Christian Ecumenism to Interfaith Dialogue

I think everyone realizes as they look at the trajectory that ecumenism expands almost naturally into interfaith work. Karl Rahner pointed out in a very famous article, "Towards a Fundamental Interpretation of Vatican II," that *Nostra Aetate* signaled that the relationship of Christianity to other faiths has become the new frontier. People who were trained as I was and learned from the Christian ecumenists how to build those bridges are drawn to building the other bridges, and the reason is this: every voyage into another Christian communion or into another faith, if it is done properly in the spirit of Lonergan—searching for truth, not thinking that you have it (who could ever have truth, for heaven's sake!)—will always or inevitably result in mutual illumination. As we find in ecumenical circles, and as part of George's testimony, and as we find in interfaith circles, you are given a richer understanding of your own faith as you try to understand others. In the world in which we live today it has become very important in neighborhoods. [People may ask,] how am I going to raise my children in this totally permissive Western society? You find out as a Muslim family moves in next to you that you are happy to find somebody who has faith! That it is a different faith is less important than that they have faith and out of that faith, they begin to raise their children—the same with Jews.

Still Learning from Aquinas and Other Friends

Aquinas is a great friend. I think going back to Aquinas has much to teach us. Here is this man in the thirteenth century who is in a culture war with the people in the arts faculty who were reading Aristotle in a quite different way. But he sees that this should not be a threat but should be a challenge to more deeply understanding his tradition. That is what Lonergan taught me.

I don't think analogy is a theory. Analogy is the way we live our lives. When Paul says, "Not I but Christ lives within me," the meaning of that word *live* has two very different senses in the same sentence. If you cannot live with that, then you better go home. It seems to me that the intellectual suppleness that a good philosophical training can give allows one to appreciate how interaction opens to friendship, because dialogue has to lead to friendship. Friendship with others allows them to give witness of their faith to you, which humbles you and as you get humbler, maybe you can give witness to your own faith.

Closing Comments

I want to agree with George Lindbeck and Joseph Ratzinger and John Howard Yoder and Stanley Hauerwas that the primary task is trying to follow Jesus. As Kierkegaard says, you can never say you are a Christian except in the banal sense of registry and always trying to become one. I think that communities like Christian theological seminaries that try to understand the world in which they live and the faith which they follow can animate our republic. But without it, we'll be stuck in culture wars, and we'll be absolutely stuck in religious debates that are pointless. To me community and the way in which those communities meld with other communities has nothing to do with relativism. Any time I meet someone of another faith, it certainly relativizes my understanding of my faith and carries it further. But it does not make everything the same or monochromatic. What happens when we meet a pluralistic environment in which we live? . . . There are many faiths, there are many traditions, and we could have two reactions. It is kind of like one's reaction to food. We each have two different reactions. Some have different reactions on different days. "I don't like it." "You haven't tried it!" "I don't like it." "Alright, let's try it." This whole sense of otherness . . . we can either respond in a welcoming posture, which is what I think our faith ought to lead us to if we are seeking understanding, or we can respond in fear if we need certitude. That is where our young people are posed today, and I think we have to help them through that maze.

5

"Blessed Are the Peacemakers, for They Shall See God"

An Interview with Stanley Hauerwas

Stanley Hauerwas represents the youngster of the three friends, even as he prepares for emeritus status at Duke Divinity School, where he has taught since he left the University of Notre Dame in 1984—the year that Professor Lindbeck published The Nature of Doctrine. *Professor Hauerwas has thereby stood bodily in the fissure between a Roman Catholic theology department and a mainline Protestant divinity school. In so doing, his life characterizes the "ecclesial wanderings" of a so-called Protestant theologian who seeks to recover resources from the Great Church tradition to renew the witness of the church catholic. By insisting on the ecclesial location for theological thought, Professor Hauerwas has received a "public" hearing that has ironically exceeded the breadth of influence of theologians who have insisted upon a "public" location for the theological*

*task precisely to gain such a hearing. Perhaps most remark-
ably, however, Professor Hauerwas has excelled throughout his
life as a teacher. He has directed over sixty PhD dissertations,
largely because students have found great support and freedom
in working under his guidance. Professor Hauerwas has recently
provided theological reflections on his life in his autobiographical memoir,* Hannah's Child.[1]

On Friendship

I hope it's Jesus that has brought me to friendship with George
and David. George and David are such accomplished people. I'm
not; I'm a Texan. English is my second language. I came into a
world that they had seen but I only read about. I come from a
different class. I was raised a bricklayer. I was the first person
in my family to go to college. I was a student of the world that
they inhabited. I think what I like about George and David is
that the world they inhabit can really be filled with bullshit.[2]
But they are non-bullshit people. And it takes a lot of training
to be trained out of bullshit.

On College

It had so much to do with education. I always say that I became
a theologian because I couldn't get saved. You were supposed to
get saved on Sunday night, and I didn't think you should fake
it, and it just never happened. So I decided to dedicate my life
to the ministry because that way, God would be indebted. And
so I dedicated my life to ministry. I was told I should read, so
I started reading. I read a book somewhere down the line by
a man named David Napier, called *From Faith to Faith*, and I
discovered that the Bible wasn't true. We weren't smart enough
to be fundamentalists, but I had thought the Bible was true. So

1. See Stanley Hauerwas, *Hannah's Child: A Theologian's Memoir* (Grand Rapids: Eerdmans, 2010).
2. See H. G. Frankfurt, *On Bullshit* (Princeton: Princeton University Press, 2005).

it was a shock to discover that it wasn't. Then I read a book by Nels F. S. Ferre called *The Sun and the Umbrella*. It suggested to me that religion probably hid God as much as revealed God, and I thought, "That's right." I gave it up. And so I went to college, because I wouldn't have gone to college if I hadn't thought at one time that I was going into the ministry.

In college I had a wonderful teacher named John Score. I was *the* philosophy major at Southwestern University in Georgetown, Texas. I took a six-semester course in the history of philosophy in which we read Copleston and the primaries. I began to understand that I wasn't smart enough to be an atheist. R. J. Collingwood was one of the main people [who was] very influential [to] me.

To Yale Divinity School

I decided to go to divinity school to discover, once and for all, if I believed this stuff. And I had read H. Richard Niebuhr's *The Meaning of Revelation*, through which I had decided history was the deciding issue. And so I decided to go to Yale; I didn't know that H. Richard had decided to retire and die. I found myself going to Yale to study with H. Richard Niebuhr, and he wasn't there. And instead, [during] my first year at Yale Divinity School, I had Brevard Childs for Pentateuch; I had Walther Zimmerli for the Prophets (I thought the prophets were Karl Barth). I had Julian Hartt for systematic theology, in which I read Austin Ferre and Karl Barth. I had Paul Holmer for Kierkegaard, and I had Ed Dirks for theology and the university. The next year I took Robert Calhoun's History of Doctrine course.[3] For the class you either took a five-hour exam on a classic text or wrote a fifty-page paper. I thought, "I ought to read the *Summa*." I just read the *Summa* and took a five-hour exam. At the same time I had Mr. Holmer's Philosophical Theology course. The first semester we read Wittgenstein's *Tractatus* and *The Blue and*

3. For the first half of Calhoun's course, with an introduction by George Lindbeck, see Calhoun, *Scripture, Creed, Theology* (Eugene, OR: Cascade, 2011).

Brown Books—this was philosophical theology! The second
semester we read the *Investigations*. So I was reading Aquinas
and Wittgenstein at the same time. And I took Hans Frei's Christology course. Mr. Frei went through the ancient christological
controversies, but we also went through Protestant liberalism.
One of the things that I was increasingly becoming aware of
was how high christological doctrine could leave out the life of
Jesus. I raised the issue of what it meant constructively to be a
sanctificationist and how discipleship was formative and shaping for what it means to be holy, for a community to be holy.

George Lindbeck was at Vatican II during a lot of this early
time. I took a course with Ian Siggins on comparative exegesis
of the Reformers. I read Luther's commentary on the Gospel
of John—three volumes—and Calvin. I learned at that time
that justification by faith was a christological move rather than
the anthropological move that so many Protestant liberals had
turned it into. I don't remember becoming a Christian; I just
found myself so compelled, particularly by Barth, into the engagement that I just knew that this is what I wanted to do with
my life. I distrust conversion language deeply because it's such
an invitation to narcissism. So I only remember that theology
gave me such an enthralling something to do. And I wanted to
do it.

What Julian Hartt had convinced me of in theology was that
it is a mistake to think of theological discourse as a kind of
primitive metaphysics. I remember Julian as a ninth-generation
Methodist. What Julian had taught me in philosophical theology
was that theological claims were fundamentally forms of practical discourse. Of course I'd picked that up from Wittgenstein
and from Aquinas through Aristotle. I just thought I was being
a good Wesleyan. And John Score, the man that I had studied
with at Southwestern College, had written his dissertation under
Bob Cushman at Duke, who had recovered Wesley in a non-
Aldersgate mode. I began to see Wesley's fundamental theological understanding to be the formation of his life through
the field preaching and the class meeting. I was beginning to
be pulled toward a richer account of the church than I had

anticipated. Somehow I was trying to put all that together. I've been trying to put it together my whole life.

The Attraction to Aquinas

I was particularly attracted to Aquinas because I was coming out of philosophy of action at that time. I saw in Aquinas the account of activity that I thought was necessary for the display of the required habits to make us virtuous. And I saw that in the habitual nature of speech. I was extraordinarily attracted to what I regarded as the investigative character of Aquinas. I just picked up the *Summa* and read it. Then I started reading Catholics on Aquinas, and I didn't know we were reading the same text. I remember reading Garrigou-Lagrange, and I thought, "Jee-sus!" I mean the great temptation is to reify categories that for Aquinas are heuristic. And so what you get with Catholics is that they are so overdetermined because they are so powerful. They have people that can grasp part of Aquinas and turn it into a lifetime's work, often scholarly [and] very impressive. But as a result, they can miss exactly the kind of investigative character of the whole enterprise.

Neither/Both Catholic and/or Protestant

When I went to Notre Dame, they asked, "What do you want to teach?" And I said, "I want to teach a seminar on the Prima Secundae and the Secunda Secundae." They said, "Oh, Aquinas is a Catholic theologian." I said, "Oh really? When did that happen? You guys didn't exist before we existed. You had to have Protestants to make you Catholic. He's sure as hell as much in my tradition as he is in yours. So I don't know why you get to claim possession."

I think that was in part the developments of the time, that the *ressourcement* movement was opening up a way. As David put it quite wonderfully, these were not historical theologians that we read about, but that we learned from. They were our friends, who we learned how to think with.

Response to Vatican II

We read the documents of Vatican II. I remember reading *De Ecclesia* quite carefully. As a matter of fact, one time George came back and I had written a paper on John Courtney Murray. George heard about it, and said that he wanted to talk to me about it. George, you probably don't remember this at all. And I was very critical of Murray because I'm a Barthian, and I thought that he was deeply deficient christologically. In the document "On Religious Liberty" the French and the Americans were at some loggerheads. I was on the French side. I remember talking about it with George, but I don't remember the conversation at all. But that was in the air. I also took a course with Eugene TeSelle on modern Catholic thought. And we went back to Maréchal. We read Maréchal, "On Nature-Grace"; we read Blondel, "Action"; we read de Lubac; I think we read Rahner. I was early on introduced to that pre–Vatican II Roman Catholic thought. My last semester when I was writing my dissertation at Yale, Bernard Haring came. I took Father Haring's class in Moral Theology. We read "The Law of Christ," which I thought was completely incoherent, and I let him know it. His judgment was that I lacked charity. It was just that time that you were beginning to get the christological return in Catholic moral theology, but in a way that "we follow Christ, but it doesn't make any difference for how we do casuistry." That was the kind of issue that I was pressing.

The Discovery of the Significance of Worship

The other part of it was, at Yale Divinity School, we went to chapel to find out what our professors were thinking if they were preaching. It never occurred to us that worship had anything to do with chapel. Somewhere down the line it occurred to me that Christians worshiped God. And I couldn't get a handle on that at all. And so, I found a book in the library by a man named Dom Gregory Dix called *The Shape of the Liturgy*. I read the book, and I thought, "Jee-sus! This liturgy stuff is really important, and I'm going to have to think about that." And so, of course, I didn't do anything about it at Yale at all. But when I went to my first teaching job at Augustana College in Rock Island, Illinois, I thought I ought to go to church. They had a wonderful campus church, and so I discovered the Green Book, the 1978 Lutheran Book of Worship. And I was very much shaped by the liturgical form that the Green Book represents. It was a wonderful sung liturgy, and the hymns are terrific.

When I left Augustana and went to South Bend—you know I'm an ecclesial whore, being a Methodist—I just thought, "Well, I've been worshiping with the Lutherans at Augustana; I'll worship with the Lutherans when I go to South Bend." When I went to Lutheran churches in South Bend, they didn't do anything like what I had been doing with the Swedish Lutherans. I asked Robert Jenson about it once, and he said, "The Reformation in Germany was a people's movement, and they just changed everything. The Reformation in the High Countries was just that the bishops decided to be Lutheran, and they just decided to do what they'd always done. So the liturgical form of the high-country Lutheranism remained more determinatively related to Catholic liturgical forms." And so the people that I could find that worshiped most nearly like what I had come to love were the Roman Catholics at Notre Dame. I went to Mass. I was raising a son under some very difficult circumstances, and David was saying Mass in Grace Hall. I don't know if David remembers this at all, but he was the rector in Grace Hall. I would bring Adam, who was two or three at the time, and he would run around and go up to the altar, and he thought little children were supposed to stand by David when he was giving the epiclesis. So I worshiped with the Roman Catholics. I was probably the most faithful attendee at Sacred Heart for a number of years. It was the liturgical shaping that was so important for me.

Early Publications

I think that I couldn't find a publisher for my dissertation, and so my first book was *Vision and Virtue*. I think I tried to get my dissertation published at Notre Dame, and Notre Dame wouldn't take it. Then I tried to publish it with a press called Corpus, which started and quickly went out of business. But they did one great thing for me. They were interested in publishing the dissertation, so they sent me the first book they had published. It was by a man named Herbert McCabe, a Dominican in New Blackfriars, Oxford, called *Law, Love, and Language*. Herbert McCabe said what I wanted to say. After reading that book, my little book seemed very little to me. But at the time that I was doing this, situation ethics was everything. And so I was just trying to change the subject; I've been trying to change the subject my whole life. I think in some ways that is what we represent. We're not trying to provide answers to old questions; we're trying to change the questions. And that takes a lot of reworking, also of yourself. I thought the focus on character and the philosophy of action and so on that I was developing was still important at that time, though I thought Herbert did it so much better than myself. People forget also that *Character and Christian Life* (my dissertation) has really an extensive account of Bultmann and how deeply I read Bultmann as providing an alternative—why I found Bultmann's form of Protestant liberalism finally so deficient. But that was so much in the air of the day; to go against it was very hard.

Appointment to Notre Dame

Notre Dame was desperate at the time to find someone to teach Christian ethics. At first they tried to attract Charlie Curran, and Charlie turned them down. And then they tried to hire a friend of mine named Jim Childress, who taught at the University of Virginia, and Jim turned them down. And so Jim Burtchaell phoned Jim Gustafson and said, "Have you got anybody else?" And he said, "Well there's this guy out at Augustana who you might want to look at." So it was just sheer contingency.

    Jim had a marriage to perform in Moline, Illinois. He had to come out there anyway, so he phoned me up and said, "Can

I talk to you?" And I said, "I would love to talk to you." I was being fired at Augustana. I told the Lutherans when I was hired there that of course as someone committed to serious moral reflection, I had to challenge the Lutheran presumption of justification being the primary doctrine. I thought that that might set them off. It turned out they didn't care any about theology, but they cared a whole lot about manners, and I didn't have any. So I got in trouble pretty quick.

So I was being fired when Jim called me up. There are these huge steps at the main entrance at Augustana. When Jim drove up I was sitting up there waiting for him in my normal attire— T-shirt, Bermuda shorts, and shoes with no socks. He later said that he got out of the car and looked up there and said, "Dear Lord, don't let that be him." But it was, and we talked. I told him that I thought most contemporary Catholic moral theology was absolutely intellectually shabby and theologically without interest, and that I thought that I had something to say. And I guess that he was intrigued enough that they brought me and interviewed me. I think that they recognized that I represented an agenda that might be constructive. So they wanted me to teach Protestant Christian ethics, and I said that is the last thing I'd be looking to teach. I wouldn't know what that looks like. And so I said I'd just teach theological ethics.

Toward the Healing of the Reformation

As Walter Cardinal Kasper says, "It's never a question of return." But it is a question of our faithfulness in Christ. And you have to be animated by the tradition. If we struggle through our parochial histories as best we can, we will discover a unity that God has given us that we have not made. George, in the lovely article he wrote in *God, Truth, and Witness: Engaging Stanley Hauerwas*, asked why I had never been interested in the ecumenical movement. I wrote him and said, "When I graduated from seminary, in America the Protestant ecumenism was, as far as I could see, denominational executives of the various

Protestant denominations trying to see how they could join their denominational headquarters under diminishing resources to discover how unity could occur without anyone losing a job." And I just wasn't interested in that.

But I am a Methodist. Methodism, of course, is an incoherent tradition because we're a movement that by accident became a church in America. If you're not overwhelmed with hunger for Christian unity as a Methodist, you don't understand who you are. So I don't know why God has made some of us ecclesially homeless in this time, but if it's to serve the quest for unity, then all has not been lost. I am an ecumenical movement. The Lutherans and the Catholics made me who I am. It's one thing to read Aquinas; it's another thing to pray with someone who reads Aquinas. I just thank God that God has pulled me into such a remarkable inter-nexus of people who have made me more than I could ever be. Of course God is having his revenge. I've spent twenty-three years now with the Methodists.

George has said in interviews lately that while he thought the loss of Christendom was good for the church, it's not particularly good for the world. I agree with that even though I'm an anti-Constantinian à la Yoder. But if it's not good for the world, one of the things that may be happening, given George's analysis, is that God is giving us a mission at this time in the world in which we find ourselves. I think that we will discover we are in more profound unity than we could ever have imagined. Our task is to be as faithful as we can be in the place we've been given.

The Influence of John Howard Yoder

John Howard Yoder is such a significant figure for David and myself. And you've got to remember that I think that the Anabaptists were not Protestant reformers; they were Catholic reformers. That sense of the community that John wouldn't let us lose, I think, is an imaginative alternative. It's real for us to rediscover in what way Christian unity isn't suddenly

Presbyterians and Methodists discovering that they don't have anything to disagree about because they didn't have anything to believe anyway. Christian unity really is, "A modest proposal for peace: let the Christians of the world resolve not to kill each other." Start there. And then you will see why you need Father, Son, and Holy Spirit, because you're going to need a lot of protection. And you're going to need to pray to the true God truly. So that's the way I think about the ecumenical passion.

Vatican II and the Church as the Messianic People of God

I think that one of the things that we need to say about Vatican II—and I'm not sure that it has been appropriately emphasized yet—is that Vatican II recovered the christological heart of the church. And that is exemplified in John Paul II. John Paul II was a christological pope from beginning to end. And the rediscovery of the absolute particularity of Jesus, of this Palestinian Jew as the Son of God, means that you are absolutely forced to be reconnected to the people of Israel, the Jews. There is absolutely no way to avoid that. Paul Minear's *Images of the Church in the New Testament* was very influential in Vatican II when they were trying to take up the question of the nature of the church. And we were all on the side of the image "the people of God," for we all thought that allegedly meant the church should be democratic and not hierarchical—what a stupid thought. Instead, how "the people of God" connected the church to the people of Israel was a crucial insight that we were learning. What Hans Frei was teaching us had to do with how Christ's life is the recapitulation of Israel's life. It was that christological focus—which, of course, Barth was so influential with too—that was pulling us deeper into this understanding of the church's relationship with Israel. And just think about Yoder's *Jewish-Christian Schism Revisited*. It's not accidental that John thought one of the decisive issues was when the church tried to universalize itself in a way that it could run an empire and therefore lost the story of Israel. So the politics of your ecclesial character vis-à-vis the world would also shape how you reconnected the story with the story of Israel. I think that is part of what we are now trying to think through, and I think George signaled that in *The Future of Roman Catholic Theology*. And I think what I learned from George and Hans set me up for Yoder, no matter how much their Niebuhrian hearts may dislike that. I mean, Reinhold Niebuhr is a lot to get over. It takes a lot of work.

But we have to be careful with the image of pilgrim or alien people. My friend Peter Ochs constantly impresses on me, you don't make exile normative. It's not for me to tell Jews to think that exile is normative. I think at least for Christians it is. Rahner's essay that David referenced on Vatican II reminded Catholics that although there are a lot of you, if you look at it from the world's perspective, you're not in control. That's a very important thing to learn. I mean it's very hard to remember that in Rome. But I think it is a lesson that Rome is learning. And we need to be all there to learn it together.

Theology as Teaching Speech

I think I'm doing theology the way theology should be done, that is, nonsystematically. This means we can somehow perhaps leave eighteenth- and nineteenth-century Germany behind. It means that you are constantly looking for ways to show how language works, to help you discover the world that you are living in, but the world that you are living in is about constant denial of the world you are living in. And so you try to provide imaginative speech proposals for how it is we need to see the world, and what are the conditions for the possibility of that seeing. So what I do is journalism. It's the attempt to provide little news articles of redescription through which the language does work. And so it never comes to an end. I'd like to say, "Oh that's what I really think" in a short way, but I can't do it because of what I think. It's very frustrating. If you've been schooled by Wittgenstein, it is all therapy, and that's what I continually try to do. And so it's true that I tell my students I don't want them to think for themselves; I want them to think like me, but I want them to know how to think like me in order to do what I do better.

Habit is everything. The scholarship provides the linguistic habits that [help us] to see the world truly rather than how it's presented to us by the forces and other things around us. I mean, theology is fundamentally teaching speech. And so you constantly try to help yourself and others with the grammar necessary not to let your language go to pot.

On Alasdair MacIntyre

A name that we haven't mentioned that has been so influential on myself is Alasdair MacIntyre. It's not at all accidental that those thinkers deeply shaped by Wittgenstein, Anscombe, Geach, MacIntyre—I'm sure I'm missing some—all went back and recovered Aristotle. It's not accidental at all. Aristotle's understanding of activity is exactly what Wittgenstein, I think, meant [when] quoting Goethe in a very different way, [who] said, "In the beginning was the deed." You don't ever look for anything deeper than what you say because in the beginning was the deed. And of course the deed was creation; we participate, and that's how we try to constantly recover that speech pattern.

On Contingency

It's contingency all the way down. The narrative, the significance of narrative, is "in the beginning God created." It doesn't get more basic than that. What Victor Preller taught us is the metaphysical significance of contingency, because if you could prove God rather than simply show how creation declares God's glory (to which Aquinas's proofs may well testify), you lose the Christian God. If you could prove God, you wouldn't need witnesses, you'd only need philosophers. But exactly because you can't prove God in that necessitating mode, God has willed to be known through us. What an extraordinary life! We stand with the people of Israel and the Son of God, the second Person of the Trinity, displaying for the world God's humanity. That's a gift that I don't think I'll ever get over.

This is exactly what I tried to say in *With the Grain of the Universe*. Its fundamental argument is that you can't have a natural theology separated from the full doctrine of God as the Father, Son, and Holy Spirit. You also need people who have learned then to live in these extraordinary ways, people like John Howard Yoder, Dorothy Day, John Paul II. And I'm well aware that John Paul II was, at least as a Pole, Constantinian all the way down. I try to narrate him as a non-Constantinian pope, but I think that that's not altogether unintelligible if Rahner is right that with Vatican II the church entered a post-Constantinian era.[4] Therefore to make John Howard Yoder and John Paul II deeper allies than most people would expect, I do not think is entirely unreasonable.

On Friendship

I can't live without friends. My life at one time, probably still today, hung on the intercessory prayers my friends made on my behalf. I think how friendship and the life of prayer are internally related to one another. It is the great gift we give people as Christians in the world in which we find ourselves. We're not friends because we're desperate, but because we share a common joy. And the world is dying for that joy. And so it's not something you do to get it; it's what we've been given. Of course, Aristotle thought only people of great virtue and character could be friends of one another. David's account of Aristotelian friendship shows that this meant people that were weak or ugly or unlucky couldn't be friends in terms of character friendship. And that's the reason why I think the work of people like Jean

4. Karl Rahner, "Towards a Fundamental Interpretation of Vatican II," *Theological Studies* 40 (1979): 716–27.

Vanier and the L'Arche movement is so important. Through such persons we learn how to become a friend of someone that we call profoundly mentally disabled, when, in fact, that person is a friend of God and therefore can be a friend, our friend. That's very threatening. You must learn the speech of the body and not be frightened by the speech of the body required to live in a L'Arche community. And so that kind of friendship that we Christians believe in is but the exemplification of the friendship that God wants us to have with one another and with God, [and this friendship] makes possible an alternative world that is *the* world. And so friendship is everything to me.

What's tricky about that is how friendship can become a substitute for the church. The church names friends I have but I do not yet know. So it is the hope that we will be united in God's life in a way that we can hardly imagine now. There are a lot of people I worship with that I really think are shits, and I really don't want to be friends with them. But I hope in the future that we will be. So it is a hard prayer that you want to be friends with some of these people. I'm sure that they don't think that about me! So I do think that friendship is very much at the heart of the gospel. You are no longer slaves; I call you my friends. John 15:15, I think, is really central.

Closing Comment

I think I'll say what John Paul II said (not that I put myself in his company). "Be not afraid." I mean, by God, we've been given a wonderful task. I think the most important thing you can do is not be afraid of speech, of fundamental Christian speech. When they say, "What do you really mean?" you have to say again, "Jesus is Lord." There's no deeper meaning than that. Let me show all the connections you need to make to live that. The problem with experiential-expressivism and cognitive propositionalism is that they imply speech is somehow deficient if you can't give it a meaning more determinative than what you said. Which means that you haven't learned what you need to say well. So it is a great gift you have been given to help people not be robbed of their speech.

An example I always give is that you oftentimes hear Americans—[especially] deeply conservative Americans—say, "Jesus is Lord, but that's just my personal opinion." Our task is to defeat that speech-act. If you can defeat that kind of speech-act, you will discover that you've made people extraordinarily happy in the Aristotelian sense. And that means that—and you're not going to believe I'm going to say this—that means you can't read the Bible enough. You can't read the Bible enough because that's where you learn the grammar. I just realized (and who could have ever anticipated that at Yale during those years—they didn't always agree, I can assure you) that you could get together Paul Holmer, George Lindbeck, Hans Frei, Mr. Meyer, Julian Hartt to give us the confidence in speech. What an extraordinary gift.

6

Israel, Judgment, and the Future of the Church Catholic

A Dialogue among Friends

The New Fragmentation of the Church

Hauerwas: I think that the division that is occurring within the churches in the current context (which is more determinative than past divisions) is a sign of the highly accommodated character of the church. It's a judgment on the lingering effects of church trying to run the world. Just to the extent that the church then loses its desire to run the world, we have a better chance to discover the unity on the other side. That little article that I wrote, "Why Gays as a Group Are Morally Superior to Christians as a Group"—it's really about that. I said, how can gays do anything so morally inventive as get themselves banned from the military as a group, and what do Christians have to do to have that happen to them? Even just warriors have to worry about where you bomb and about military strategies. And that kind of thing is not good for the military. Or that Christians always think you should tell the truth, even to the enemy. Do national militaries really want that? Christians think that they should pray for their enemy. Christians don't think that they can kill on the day they receive the body and blood of their Lord. They were an evangelizing sect. Would you want to shower with them? You never know when they are going to lay baptism on you. Why can't Christians get themselves banned from the military as a group?

Now if we were a people so suspected by the world that we couldn't be in the United States military, would gays want to be part of the church? And if they did, we could say, "We're not really interested in your sexuality, whether it's fulfilled or not—we've got bigger things at stake." So if Christians could recover that sense, dare I say, of holiness, then I think we would discover we shared more with other Christians than we thought, because the gay issue would be entirely reconfigured. That's the way that I think about it; it may be fantasy, but you've got to start somewhere.

Burrell: I want to talk a little bit about the church in the Holy Land where I live, and what I've learned about being a Christian there. George has been to our ecumenical institute, which sits on the seam between Bethlehem and Jerusalem. We have a wonderful Anglican canon by the name of Naim Sabiq. He directs an Arabic group called "The Path," which has been influenced by Palestinian liberation theology. He does what he does very well, but it doesn't quite fit; it is obviously an import from Latin America. We had a young Czech woman who was doing an inquiry and asked, "What kind of theology would emerge from the church in the situation in which it is in the Holy Land?" When Paul VI asked Father Hesburgh to start an ecumenical institute in Jerusalem, as Paul VI put it, "where we were all once one," he was shrewd enough to know that Christians are more divided in Jerusalem than anywhere else in the world. So it's also a challenge. Every time we go through the Christian unity week there with all these guys in funny dress, it looks like a charade to me.

But we must talk about something deeper. Christians in the Holy Land are a minority, a powerless minority in the land where Jesus lived—ain't that a humiliation? As much as I've signed on through Stanley to John Howard Yoder's thing that we shouldn't have the power, I want it. Alex Awad, the Palestinian dean at the Bethlehem Bible College, can't travel to Jerusalem because he doesn't have the right papers. I said, "Alex, what's it like?" And he said, "Well, it's kind of like Jesus, isn't it?" I said, "Okay." That's how Baptists can keep you straight sometimes.

It's another take on what Stanley said. I just wanted to contextualize it. We need one another desperately, and therefore we have a great deal to learn from one another. It isn't that we try to erase our differences. Our differences are very helpful. The God that we worship is beyond our conceptualization anyways, so different ways to that God are certainly going to illuminate and enlighten us. But more particularly we need strength to walk in a world that marginalizes us; and if it doesn't marginalize us, it's even worse. Because one of the things that I think is that late capitalism is more dangerous to Christianity than Marxism. Marxism dominated the church from the outside; late capitalism eats out its guts from the inside and turns it into part of the market society. Wherever we are, people are becoming more and more conscious of their need for faith. And this faith will express itself in different Christian groups; it will express itself across other faith divides because they are talking about faith. Fundamentally what I have learned in the years I lived through the Intifada and Holy Land, is . . . to try and trade in my native American optimism [for it to] be transformed into hope. We Americans are born with optimism because we had this empty (was it empty?) continent to exploit, and we always had a frontier ahead of us. As the Americans in the Second [World] War always said, "The impossible takes a little longer." Best example of this that I can [think of happened] as I'm riding my bicycle on a major street at a quarter of six in the morning to go off swimming. In Beth Sahour we have a YMCA pool; I go there three mornings a week. There's a BMW pulled off the side of the road, and it's one of my swimming partners. I pull to the side, and I say, "What's that?" "It's a puncture." I said, "Let's fix it." As a driver of a BMW, my friend had never fixed a tire in his life. And that's the American strength, "Let's fix it." That's also what we've done in Baghdad. The Greek tragedies tell us that a person's strengths are also his weaknesses. Optimism can lead very quickly to riding roughshod over others; hope means that we know that we are inadequate to the task. We have to trust in the presence of the Spirit of Jesus.

Lindbeck: I'm going to talk about a difficulty as I was listening to others. This is a sign, I think, of having grown up abroad for the first seventeen years of my life. I felt more like an alien when I first came to the United States to go to college than I've ever felt anywhere, at any time since. The first year of college was absolutely the worst year of my life. I scarcely remember anything about it; I knew nobody. Everyone took me for an American because I spoke like an American; I looked like an American. I didn't understand anything that they were saying, [I wanted] nothing that they were wanting.

At any rate, I'm not the fixer type. That amused me about Americans from the very beginning. I had never driven a car; I had never tried to fix an engine or do anything at all with a car. I've learned a few of those things, but I wouldn't have if I hadn't lived in America. But one of the things that badly needs to be fixed in the ecumenical movement can't be done by human power. Congar quoted C. S. Lewis several times that those who are really good ecumenists are those who live most deeply into the depths of their own tradition. And this is one of the horrors of being a divided church. One meets Christ in all our traditions, in all traditions that are rooted in historic Christianity. One meets Christ most deeply when one moves into a particular form of Christianity. And the church is historically concrete; it exists only in historically concrete bodies, and those bodies are now historically divided. And they are divided against each other inevitably. To be a Lutheran is not to be a Catholic, and for most of the world, that's the most important thing about it. We've already seen examples of what Ephraim Radner calls "contrastive identities," . . . [for example] in the list of the most important Catholic doctrines that David earlier referred to from the 1907 book [*The Fundamentals of Catholic Teaching*].

But nevertheless we have been given the possibility of meeting. This is what was so wonderful about the Second Vatican Council. Almost all of those observers were drawn from the people who were really genuinely committed to ecumenism. And so we found that we could meet together and feel a deep sense of fellowship precisely because of the centrality and importance of Jesus Christ and the God known in and through Jesus Christ for us. And what's happening now, what's been happening through the last half century in all our traditions—including, as I understand, the Nazarenes as much as anyone else—is a loss of that depth, that identity, with the result that fewer and fewer of the children growing up in our churches actually live into the depths of their tradition. And in a peculiar type of way this results in many cases in a kind of reaction. What really is distinctive about our particular version of Christianity? And you can't feel committed to Christianity at all unless you are committed to a concrete people. I've seen this through decades of teaching a diversity of Roman Catholics and any number of different Protestant groups. One advantage in a place like Yale Divinity School was students would come to us with empty minds, willing to be filled with whatever we gave them, to much a greater degree than in the past. But that, of course, is the kind of thing that you don't want to happen. You want some resistance. Then the learning might really amount to something; it is not simply to be a matter of needing certitude but rather seeking understanding.

What the good God is doing to the church, it seems to me, is destroying us bit by bit. And I think that God insists God wants us to be united. And destroying each denomination's identity is precisely the way in which eventually we'll have to be united. But, nevertheless, if you are going to be really ecumenical, you are going to have to know your own tradition and love it to its depths. I don't know what that means in Nazarene terms, but for those of you who are Nazarene, I've discovered one wonderful thing about [it] in the last day—namely, that you are trying to keep together internationally. Outside of the Roman Catholics, the

Nazarenes are the only ones who are trying to keep together internationally. I hope that you succeed, and I hope that you succeed even if this means that Americans become a minority and have to let newer and newer mission extensions of the Nazarenes be the dominant group. If you succeed in that you will be doing the type of Christian sacrifice that brings us closer to Christ.

Ecumenism and Recapturing the Jewish Roots of the Messianic People of God

Lindbeck: One of the things that I've discovered as a student of the history of Christian thought is that the church as Israel was really very important in constructive ways for the church for the first fifteen centuries. Now it was not equally constructive; sometimes it was disastrous. But Christians really thought that they were Israel—sometimes in a disastrous sort of way, because they thought that the Jews were no longer Israel. But nevertheless this meant that they took their unity, even after the Reformation, seriously. When they talked about Christendom, they did not think of what we think of as Christendom. They thought that we are all baptized into the same faith and that we really do belong together, even though we are divided. To some extent the Reformed are an exception. Shortly after the Reformation, more and more on all sides, both Protestants and Catholics, forgot about the church being Israel. It happened three or four centuries ago to a remarkable extent. The church became defined more and more by contrastive identities, what differentiates us from others, the Catholics, the Protestants. And so they no longer talked about the church as Israel or thought about the church as Israel. That sense of a unity—sometimes it was very much a sociological unity—tended to disappear. The sense of a common peoplehood, transcending cultures and boundaries, seems to me to exist much more strongly in Roman Catholicism than it does in any branch of Protestantism. Anglicans have a little bit of it, not much; I wish they had more. What we need to do is to find out that we are indeed one people, the people of Israel, as an interlocking part of the Jews as Israel. It is a very difficult thing to do. In other words, we have to be nonsupersessionist; we don't replace Israel. We're in the very strange position of being part of the chosen people of God, even while there is another branch of the chosen people of God, most of whom do not accept Jesus Christ as Savior. That relationship is extraordinarily awkward. Now we are getting messianic Jews, real Jews, and some of them are even becoming completely Torah-observant. And nevertheless they confess that Jesus is the Messiah. And to accept them as really Christians is extraordinarily difficult; it puts enormous strains on the relationship with Jews, many of whom I and David and Stanley have very close relations with. I don't know how it will work, but I can easily conceive of struggling with the problem of how to be related to the Jews, including Christian Jews, who continue to be Jews in the full sense; I suppose that it might be one of the ways that we are forced to come together more as Christians.

It's extraordinary to me the way in which Jews want to talk to Roman Catholics; they really aren't very much interested in dialogues with Protestants. And those of us who are interested in dialogues with Jews should gather together with the Roman Catholics. There are many ways that we should be doing things together that we could do together.

Burrell: I think that there is an internal connection in the rhythms of the Shabbat, which I experienced when

I first went to Jerusalem in 1975—in the Friday evening traffic slowing down and the people stopping to
take flowers home, and the Friday evening Sabbath
ceremony, and in the Sabbath rest, which, of course,
was bowdlerized by the Reformed people (the kids
are bored on Sundays; they have to sit around in their
Sunday best). That's not the way it is at all [for Jews].
Children play, parents talk, people don't drive cars.
Fundamentally the Sabbath rules are that in Genesis 1
God created the universe well ordered but imperfect.
Our job is to perfect it. One day a week, given the
kind of beings we are, we have to quit perfecting it
to notice that we didn't in fact create it. You know,
it keeps on going without us. So it's really a deeply
communal contemplation of the gift of creation.

Now, how is it that we as Christians can appropriate some of that? In my own life, . . . from the very
first summer that I spent there thirty years ago, I've
always done that on Sunday. So I never do any work
on Sunday. I take time to be with friends on Sunday,
because if we don't do that, our psychology is so deep,
we forget to give thanks to the Lord for everything
that we see during the week. There's something utterly deep and transformative about the attitude to
time in the original covenant. And also, as George
was suggesting, we have to note how the Jews have
stuck together.

Now it goes without saying that the Zionist ven-
ture in the state of Israel has skewed our and the
Jews' perspective of Judaism in a dreadful way. The
best way to explain that is [by the example of] my
childhood friend who I was just with in Washington,
DC. He spent all his life in the CIA. His grandfather was a Reformed rabbi in Cleveland who said he
was anti-Zionist in the '30s. I said, "How can you
be anti-Zionist in the '30s?" He said, "Very simple.
We get a Jewish state; we get Jewish tanks. Jewish

tanks do what all tanks do. What's going to happen to the rest of us Jews?" In other words, the tendency of Jews now, like Americans, is to rest their hope in military power rather than in the power of God. But an increasingly large number of American Jews are realizing, as we work our way into the fortieth year of the occupation, that the occupation is killing Jews. It's killing Israelis as well as Palestinians; it's killing everything in its wake. And so we can't be romantic about our relationship to Israel, but we and Israel can help each other be faithful to the covenant that's been given to us.

Hauerwas: I don't have any great insight about these matters. I do think that one of the things that would be extremely useful is [thinking about] how reading the Old Testament helps us read the condition of the church today. And I don't think we're very good at that. Now that I'm a major biblical scholar, having written a commentary on the Gospel of Matthew . . . in the sermon "There's Not a Jot or Tittle," I refused to use the exegetical move, the distinctions between the moral law, the ceremonial law, and the juridical law as a way to avoid the question of what parts of the Torah we get to avoid. And what I had to say was that I think that Christians can no longer be protected from Jewish questions about that. I don't know how to answer them; it's difficult. But we have to remember that Leviticus is the book of holiness.

You know where the rubber hits the road really is the Shabbat. This day, and of course the resurrection day, transformed the calendar. What that means for how you read the Old Testament is just crucial. [To] narrate the Reformation in the light of the division of the kingdoms would be quite a possibility, but we don't know quite how to do it. Those are the kinds of challenges before us.

Important Predecessors to a Christologically Based Ecumenical Movement

Burrell: For the return to the christological center of the catholic faith, the *ressourcement* was the key. Look, we got embarrassed by the Reformation/Counter-Reformation dialectic, which was just silly. I gave the example of the silliness in this 1907 book on *The Fundamentals of Catholic Teaching*. We know we come from a much deeper, much richer tradition, and the newer traditions from a Catholic point of view that have come along after the Reformation have taught us something very important—[that we can] learn important things from one another, to learn for example that what went on before the Reformation is not just the history of Christian thought but vibrant, living theology.

What happens is that the boundaries become less important at the same time that it's important that one adhere to a particular way of worshiping God. So it's not that you blur the boundaries and try to create an ecumenical pastor or something, but rather that the sense of difference is less important. I love to take people to Bethlehem University. Bethlehem University is a Catholic university in Bethlehem with twenty-five hundred students, 71 percent of whom are Muslims, and 62 percent of the student body are women. And I love to see these Christian women who are dressed as Western girls walking hand in hand with a Muslim woman with modest dress from head to toe. The Christian, of course, is probably wearing a cross, but that's just to show she's not a Muslim. So there we are. I mean the signs of these are going to be identity signs, but at the same time they are reaching across those otherwise strict sociological boundaries to have friendships. So I think that that's a crucial thing.

Hauerwas: I think that one reason we saw an emergence of christologically centered ecumenism is that Karl Barth happened. I think it's a damned miracle. I don't know where in the hell he came from. But he happened. And part of what happened is that Hans Frei received him. And that was almost an equal miracle because Barth was not received in America, and yet Hans received him. And Hans taught us how to read him. And that was just an extraordinary event—chutzpah all the way down.

Burrell: And John XXIII happened. Do you know the stories of John XXIII as papal nuncio to Romania during the Phoney War? The Phoney War was the period between when the Second World War was declared in 1939 and when the fighting began in 1940, while the Germans were still building up their war machine. While John XXIII was still Angelo Roncalli, he approached the Chief Rabbi in Bucharest and said, "If you need any baptismal certificates, let me know how many you need." The Chief Rabbi was first offended about the offer of baptism. Roncalli said, "Baptism? I didn't say anything about baptism." In other words, these are people who understood how to use their faith position to help others who are in dire straits. So there were people who were known through their faith in Jesus finally who used their ecclesial power, or such as they had. And we've seen this over and again in remarkable cases, and you see it in the mission field all the time.

Lindbeck: Hans Frei, who we haven't mentioned very often, was the most important figure for what I've become, and maybe perhaps Stan would say so for himself. I'm not going to go into details about that. But rather I want to talk about the background for people like Hans Frei, like Barth himself, like the early ecumenical discussions which really moved as far as ecumenical discussions ever have. Things were as far along by 1968 as they are now in terms of the conversations that were going on, or even further. Some important or substantive things have come out much later than 1968, such as *Baptism, Eucharist, and Ministry* from the WCC in 1982 and the Joint Declaration between Catholics and Lutherans in 1999. But such things were all just commonplaces twenty years before within the ecumenical dialogue. And one of the things that made them possible was historical-critical work. Barth, who was well aware of and polemicized against biblical interpretation that limited itself to the historical-critical, nevertheless was totally at home with the method. Take something like my own teacher, my own *Doktorvater*, the director of my dissertation. Take Robert Calhoun. Calhoun called himself liberal until the time he died, but he was a liberal who actually ended up being more orthodox doctrinally than someone like H. Richard Niebuhr. Why? Because he was a historical-critical historian who was teaching a diverse group of students from many different denominations. He acted in [such] a way [that] we didn't know—if you just listened to him while you were in his class—whether he was Protestant or Catholic. He always gave an understanding from the inside of each of the people he dealt with with historical finesse and knowledge. The result was that you got what felt like a sympathetic picture, because it was from the inside, explaining why Irenaeus thought the way he did; Tertullian, the way he did; Origen, the way he did. And so on. So when you came to the condemnations of Origen, for example, a few hundred years later, you'd understand why Origen had been so misunderstood, and you're not alienated from the people who had condemned him. Of course you discovered that before Nicaea and before Chalcedon, everyone was a heretic, but you understood why they hadn't met the kinds of problems that required them to make the decisions that came with Nicaea and Chalcedon on the Trinity and the two natures of Christ. Calhoun told the story in such a way that you could be a Unitarian. I knew some Unitarians in his class who didn't think that he was trying to make them into trinitarians, but nevertheless the story that he told about trinitarian doctrines, christological doctrines, made sense to them. So if a student wanted to believe these things, they knew that they were being intellectually thoroughly respectable. The development made sense, even though you didn't have the feeling that he was trying to convert you. It was the historical method used in such a way that supported doctrinal development rather than attacking it. And the kind of thing that he did for me and for many other people allowed us to become ecumenicists. This was a superb use of the modern scientific approach. Now you have to go beyond this to include the patristic approach, and the typological also has a place. But I will say this much in appreciation of Calhoun, and in defense of modernity.

Hauerwas: Mr. Calhoun was so concerned that some of us were too much under the influence of Barth, he offered a course on F. R. Tennant. And so I spent a semester reading F. R. Tennant with Bob Calhoun trying to cure us of our Barthianism.

The Continued Constantinian Temptation

Lindbeck: Certain types of evangelicals are the most Constantinian people around. And then I listen to televangelists. All of them call themselves evangelical, and then I listen to the appeals for money. They say, "You'll get such and such if you ask for prayer"; "We'll pray for you if you give so and so." It's worse than anything against which Luther was contending, so far as the sale of indulgences was concerned. And these people call themselves the heirs of Luther. And then it's combined with this mindless patriotism, as if the United States of America were the church—and I think it is for them, at least emotionally. And all of them claim to be believers in what they call the old-time gospel. As far as terminology and verbal affirmations are concerned, I'm very much more in agreement with them than I am with people on my left. But which, the right or the left, is betraying the gospel more, I don't know. Well, as far as that goes, I'm betraying the gospel too in more subtle ways perhaps, nevertheless in genuine ways. I think we all need to repent. Repentance doesn't mean silence, and I think that ultimately Gamaliel gave us the right advice, even though he was a Jew who never became a Christian: "If this thing is of the Lord, it will last."

The high peak of ecumenical movement took place at the Second Vatican Council. I say the high peak because, just think of it, invited observers, chosen and sent by other churches, were given entrance into the inner circles of the Roman Catholic Church. Their advice was listened to. It was a kind of ecumenism on the part of the official church, by far the largest church in Christendom, a warmth of reception, a hospitality of reception, a carefulness of reception, which represented an act of unity such as never occurred before and has never occurred afterward. That's why I call it the high peak. What needs to be added . . . is that [ecumenism's] success beyond its inner circles, on both Catholic and Protestant sides . . . was supported by totally nontheological forces; the fight against communism made ecumenism seem like a very desirable thing to the Western world as a whole. The church should get together to support us more effectively in the fight against communism. The major cause, it seems to me in retrospect, for the widespread popularity [was that] the *New York Times* and *Time* magazine would be filled with news of the ecumenical council. And Lord knows, it won't be very long before totally nontheological reasons will again become very popular, and God save us from that moment. And maybe God will! Maybe something good will come out of that too. Who knows? If it's the Lord's work, it will last.

Burrell: A counterpoint to our pessimism comes from a man named James Allison, a theologian from England. He is a young man who is gay but does not write gay theology—he writes what his perspective on faith is from being gay. He is a marvelous reader of Scripture and he has an essay in which he compares the situation in which we stand now with Jesus's situation. He says, "You know, Jesus spent a lot of time in Jerusalem. It's amazing how little he talked about this imposing edifice that was right in the middle of it, the Temple. Maybe it was because the early church grew up in a collapsing Temple." Maybe that's where we are now.

Beyond the Marketplace to Signs of Hope

Hauerwas: There are some dangers still in George's response that the deeper you are in your own tradition, the deeper you are compelled to be in relation to others. How many Nazarene churches are built on holiness? I mean, it's a friendly group of people. I just wonder what it would mean for the churches to try to recover their particularity in order to renew themselves. I would like to think that would be a very good thing to do. But you live in a market-share context where churches only want to be different in order to get their market shares. And these differences rarely have to do with the battles of the past. The Nazarenes split from the Methodists with the claim that the Nazarenes were the true sanctificationalists—who's going to reproduce that today? I often think about free-will Baptists. Do you really want to reprise the issue of free will? So I worry about the fetishization about past differences in order to renew who we need to be today. I say that I have discovered what a Marxist fetish looks like. It's Methodists studying Wesley. Let's face it. Wesley was pretty boring. As much as I've learned and like to think of myself as a Wesleyan, I just don't know that moving in those directions is going to be the way forward.

I think the Lutherans and the Calvinists have a particular burden because Luther and Calvin were such impressive people; Wesley just wasn't that type of impressive guy. So you need to look elsewhere, and that's good. Now that I'm an Anglican, it's really wonderful to be in a church that has Henry VIII as its founder. You sure as hell better hope that there were better sources. It's enough to drive you back to Irenaeus. These are just musings. I just don't know really what it means to try to go back and reclaim in that way.

Burrell: Obviously, as you are saying, those things were necessary to do because there were misunderstandings that had to be disentangled. It seems to me that kind of witness we're looking for today is the witness that astounded the American people with the Amish in Pennsylvania as they forgave the murderer of their children.[1] Absolutely astounded, the American people and even the media were reduced to silence. Forgive the murderers of your children?

1. Burrell here references the tragic shooting of children in Nickel Mines, Pennsylvania, on October 2, 2006, and the community's public declaration of forgiveness of the murderer, Charles Carl Roberts IV, and their comforting his family in light of his suicide.

Lindbeck: And . . . the American culture has become de-Christianized, even while we have a society in which a great majority believes in God. I heard a report on public radio about a woman talking about how remarkable it was that the Amish, even though they were so religious, still wanted to forgive.

Burrell: That's actually quite marvelous, for it shows what the public picture of us often is.

Hauerwas: I get the *Mennonite Weekly*, and there's a headline in one of the most recent newspapers that says, "World Fascinated by Forgiveness." And I worry about that. Just to the extent that forgiveness becomes a kind of new mechanism for attention, it's no longer forgiveness. The Amish weren't doing something different from what they thought they always do. So it's very tricky. Matthew 18, which is the heart of their life, states that you are to confront the one who has sinned against you; you don't get to think about it, you're obligated to do it. That obligation is christologically determined in a way that's not for some other result. How to sustain that is absolutely crucial.

Burrell: There are other signs. The Monastic Community of Jerusalem in Paris has a church on the other side of the Seine from Notre Dame; the Community of Sant' Egidio in Rome has a church in Trastevere. Each of them has an evening prayer at 8:30 p.m. every evening, and people flock to the services. What does that say? How does evening prayer gather a community? What does it do? That's just an example. I know that the Community of Sant' Egidio also ended up brokering the peace in Mozambique. They tried to broker the peace in Algeria. When they met the Algerian rebels, the radical Islamic Salvation Front, at the airport, they said, "Look, we'd like to give you hospitality here this evening. We know what hospitality means to your culture. But we can't because this is our evening on the food line in Rome. Would you like to join us?" Well, these rebel leaders who always travel first class were really quite put on the spot, so they joined them. They found out that 70 percent of the people they were feeding were Muslims, so they won their trust for the next day in their discussions. In other words, there are things that are happening on the ground of that sort that give witness to the gospel.

Hauerwas: I think that the worry would be that I think there's nothing more important than good work done together. It was just a deep mistake to put faith and order against works in the old World Council of Churches. What worries me about that is that you might get that kind of division. And then you would not be doing anyone any good.

Burrell: It's hard to get that division if you are praying together, though.

Hauerwas: It is. I remember once, David, when we were in Paris, you took Paula and me to that Community of Jerusalem. And it's extraordinary worship.

A Last Word

Lindbeck: I'm going to make a book pitch. Stan wrote a little devotional book on the seven last words, which is unlike anything that he has written before and which moved me deeply.[2] He taught me some things about the seven last words, some mistakes I've made in understanding them, mistakes I've been making all my life. One of them is the cry of dereliction, "My God, my God, why have you forsaken me?" I've always understood

2. Stanley Hauerwas, *Cross-Shattered Christ: Meditations on the Seven Last Words* (Grand Rapids: Brazos, 2005).

that as a sort of assurance that God indeed in Jesus Christ has suffered from being deserted by God just as I have. Now I'm not going to tell you what it really means, and I don't suppose that Stan has taught us what it really means. But it's much better than that. What struck me about that was, here was someone who has not been active in the ecumenical movement in the formal sense. It's a deeply ecumenical work; it seems to me that if you read it, you wouldn't be sure if it was a Roman Catholic, an Eastern Orthodox, or a Protestant who had written it. And that kind of ecumenism can of course grow without anybody ever being involved in any formal ecumenical work. Nevertheless, formal ecumenical work is what makes that kind of ecumenical work more possible than it would otherwise be.

The trouble with any organized movement is bureaucracy. And the first generation of bureaucrats are likely to be very good, but more and more, the longer a thing lasts, the longer the generations last, the more the bureaucrats become people who are interested in moving up in the bureaucratic ladders. Any movement that gets organized has to be fed constantly from the grassroots, or things happen to it such [as what] has happened to the World Council of Churches, for example. The same is in danger of happening now in bilateral dialogues. I've met a religious affairs officer, a young man, who told me quite blandly, "Well, I've taken this job because it looked like a good way of getting a promotion."

7

Conclusion

The Appeal of the Witnesses

In the late winter of the Jubilee year, 2000, Yale University Divinity School and the Berkeley Divinity School at Yale sponsored a theology conference. The conference celebrated the Joint Declaration on the Doctrine of Justification by the Lutheran World Federation and the Roman Catholic Church, signed on October 31, 1999. The event, however, did not seem to be without its detractors. George Lindbeck gave an opening address. He had spent nearly sixty years of his life around and in the divinity school and had given himself selflessly to the work resulting in the declaration. With an irenic patience honed from years of ecumenical exchange, Lindbeck spoke to the situation:

> A good many people have expressed puzzlement over why Yale Divinity School, a university wholly independent of any Church body, should be sponsoring a conference that seems to them more ecclesiastical than academic. . . . To be sure, it is advertised as

an ecumenical rather than denominational event, but the ecumenism with which it is concerned is itself ecclesiastical, for it
has to do with the official relations of organized Church bodies. That is enough to make it "sectarian" in the way in which
Americans now use the word.[1]

At the very point where his professional life intersected with
the institutional context of his teaching career, Lindbeck found
himself enduring accusations of "sectarianism" for his work of
moving the church toward visible unity for the sake of its witness
to the world. In light of the introductory chapters, interviews,
and dialogues presented above, the accusation is profoundly
ironic, though perhaps understandable.

As the interviews have shown, Lindbeck's, Burrell's, and
Hauerwas's pursuits of their theological programs have not
been without trials—trials they still endure in order to sustain
and clarify the language and practices of the church for the
sake of its embodied witness to the world. As their dialogue
concerning the ecumenical future has shown, their endurance
has not left them bereft of hope. Years of trial and endurance,
however, have given them a hope that does not ultimately lie in
their intellectual acumen, their professional accomplishments,
or the immanent movement of the Spirit in history. Instead,
their hope is only in the Triune God. Such hope renders intelligible Lindbeck's continued advocacy for "unitive ecumenism,"
Burrell's movement from Palestine to Uganda to live amid Mus-
lim/Catholic tensions, and Hauerwas's active work to eliminate
war—activities continued long after each would be eligible to
collect their Social Security checks in peace. Their active lives
in the world do not sound like a "sectarian" withdrawal from
the world into an isolated missionary compound. Nonetheless,
the accusation persists.

Paul DeHart has recently submitted the postliberals, particularly Lindbeck, to a trial, in several senses of the word: "First,

---

1. George Lindbeck, "The University and Ecumenism," in *Justification and the
Future of the Ecumenical Movement: The Joint Declaration on the Doctrine of Justification*, ed. William G. Rusch (Collegeville, MN: Liturgical Press, 2003), 1.

a trial is a situation demanding patience or endurance. Second, to undergo a trial is to be submitted to the judgment of a public of some sort. Third, one can engage in a trial in the sense of testing or 'trying' something (or oneself) through a tentative process, an experiment."[2] DeHart finds "postliberals" success-fully passing the trial of endurance; he finds their faithfulness to the Christian tradition profoundly admirable and essential for the church. As an experiment, and especially in submission to judgment by "a public," however, DeHart finds Lindbeck and his followers (i.e., Hauerwas) severely wanting (Burrell remains off DeHart's postliberal radar).

According to DeHart, Lindbeck fails the experimental trial "about the Christian witness involving 'bringing Christ to life in the world.'"[3] DeHart abstracts Lindbeck's notion of inter-textuality from its Thomistic background and its ecumenical concerns and reads it as a universal theological method for ecclesial self-enclosure. Thus, DeHart finds a deeper failure in the "postliberal" program: Lindbeck refuses to submit Chris-tian theological claims to "the judgment of the world, but also by means of this a submission to the judgment of God's living Spirit."[4] Without this "judgment of a public of some sort," DeHart fears that "Lindbeck's cult groups would tend toward withdrawal into self-protective enclaves."[5]

The interviews and ecumenical dialogue recorded above do not indicate that Lindbeck, Burrell, or Hauerwas would lead a group into a fortified, armed communal compound awaiting apocalyptic announcements (though one never knows, particu-larly with Texans!). Perhaps an appeal to a higher court than that provided by a United States Supreme Court justice is in order. How would the witnesses fare when their accomplish-ments are placed within the context of the work for the visible unity of the church catholic, as a means of updating the faith through a return to its sources, a work that has its ties in the

2. DeHart, *Trial of the Witnesses*, 244.
3. Ibid., 260.
4. Ibid., 262.
5. Ibid., 278.

mid-twentieth-century ecumenical renewal movement that was ultimately manifested in Vatican II?

The Experiment

There is no doubt that Lindbeck, Burrell, and Hauerwas have engaged in related, though by no means identical, theological experiments. They have striven to provide textual resources for the renewal of the church catholic in the world through its local manifestations. They have recognized that the church's language is necessary to sustain the intelligibility of its practices, even as other practices render its language meaningful. They have argued in word and deed that Christ does not come to the world as a conceptual abstraction or in a mediating category, but in the concrete—but now fragmented—body of Christ and the individual bodies that comprise it. This fragmentation in the church deeply impairs the coming of Christ into the world as the Prince of Peace. The fragmented body of Christ does not provide a visible sign appropriate to the unity of love that is the Triune God.

The "contemporary" state of affairs makes it too easy for the church to be pulled into the violence of the nation-states, rather than to stand unified to show that there are other ways than killing for humans to settle their differences. Lindbeck, Burrell, and Hauerwas's work has sought to reach out to local churches and give warrants for congregations to embrace a catholicity that transcends the contemporary spatial and temporal dispersion of the body of Christ. Sustained by a tradition-based rationality, they have sought to retrieve historical witnesses and bring them into dialogue with the best of contemporary thought. Lindbeck, Burrell, and Hauerwas have all expanded theological discourse beyond the institutionally shaped discourses of the twentieth and twenty-first centuries: Lindbeck across the lines demarcated by the Reformation; Burrell across the lines between the church, synagogue, and mosque; and Hauerwas across lines determined by the contemporary liberal nation-state. Their experiments have always looked to transcend artificially constructed ecclesial, institutional, or political boundaries in order to help the "bride of Christ" to appear in her peaceful beauty within the world. In their commitment to the catholicity of the church, they have challenged the sectarian isolation formed by warring nation-states that twentieth- and twenty-first-century humans have become accustomed to accepting as natural.

One document provides evidence of their experiment, directly for Lindbeck[6] and indirectly for Hauerwas and Burrell: the Joint Declaration on the Doctrine of Justification by the World Lutheran Organization and the Roman Catholic Church. This document works for the visible unity of the church catholic as a sacrament to the world; in it, the visible unity of the church is not a means for mission; it *is* the mission to which God has called all humanity through Jesus Christ by the Holy Spirit.

In 1972 George Lindbeck gave the Père Marquette Lecture in Theology at Marquette University.[7] It is not hard to move from Lindbeck's discussion of doctrinal infallibility to the form and substance of the Joint Declaration. In the lecture Lindbeck looks for a both/and; he says that "one might argue with deliberate but perhaps excessive and misleading provocativeness that, for the sake of the non-Catholic as well as the Catholic, *Romanitas*

---

6. John A. Radano, in *Lutheran and Catholic Reconciliation on Justification* (Grand Rapids: Eerdmans, 2009), writes,

> Some observers were effective in fostering Lutheran-Catholic relationships after the Council. Some took part in the formal dialogue between the LWF [Lutheran World Federation] and the Catholic Church that began in 1967, helping to produce several of the reports instrumental in leading to the Joint Declaration, and/or in shaping the formulations within the Joint Declaration. In this sense, they were part of a process leading directly from the Second Vatican Council to the Joint Declaration, even if they did not participate personally in drafting the JD in the 1990s. Thus, George Lindbeck and Vilmos Vajta took part in the first phase of international dialogue, as member and consultant respectively, which produced the Malta Report. Lindbeck was co-chairman of the second phase, which produced All Under One Christ, and several other reports that received and applied the Malta's Report's claim of a "far-reaching consensus" on justification. . . . Lindbeck had an important role also in the American Lutheran-Catholic dialogue when it produced Justification by Faith (1985). (189–90)

7. George A. Lindbeck, *Infallibility* (Milwaukee: Marquette University Press, 1972).

needs to be retained even while infallibilism is profoundly transformed in order to remove its objectionable features."[8] From his
immersion in the medieval quaestionis form, Lindbeck notes
that especially in theological language, strict contradiction is
actually hard to achieve:

> Contradictory propositions, we recall, must be taken in precisely
> the same sense, and this has never been easy to establish even
> within the context of rationalistic theories of meaning. . . . They
> are further intensified in the light of contemporary linguistic
> philosophy with its emphasis on meaning as a function of use
> and context, and these problems are again multiplied by the
> historians' and cultural anthropologists' insights into the mu-
> tability and pluralism of intellectual, religious, and psychosocial
> situations.[9]

Linguistic therapy makes it possible to unwind previous conflict
and reframe discussion so that we might achieve a new agreement without renunciation of past theological positions: "one
can conceive of a new hermeneutical setting, different from
past and present ones, in which the doctrinal propositions on
infallibility which can be abstracted from the traditional teaching of the two confessions would no longer be incompatible."[10]
Whereas Lindbeck achieves this abstractly in his lecture on infallibility, his experiment succeeds in a church-unifying manner in the Joint Declaration at the agreed-upon crux for the
Reformation.

The Joint Declaration removes Reformation and Counter-
Reformation affirmations from their polemical setting, and
recasts them within an explicitly trinitarian setting:

> In faith we together hold the conviction that justification is
> the work of the triune God. The Father sent his Son into the
> world to save sinners. The foundation and presupposition
> of justification is the incarnation, death, and resurrection of

8. Ibid., 8.
9. Ibid., 12–13.
10. Ibid., 60.

Christ. Justification thus means that Christ himself is our righteousness, in which we share through the Holy Spirit in accord with the will of the Father. Together we confess: By grace alone, in faith in Christ's saving work and not because of any merit on our part, we are accepted by God and receive the Holy Spirit, who renews our hearts while equipping and calling us to good works.[11] (par. 15)

Based upon this new framework, the declaration reorders earlier Lutheran and Roman Catholic teachings so that they are complementary rather than contrastive in their explication of the common understanding of justification. The form modifies the Thomistic dialectic. The common confession (the solution) now orders the historic Lutheran and Roman Catholic statements as affirmative and contrastive statements, now made complementary by the common confession. Lindbeck's experiment reaches out and embraces the framework of a common catholicity.

Although not directly involved in the work of the declaration, Hauerwas's experiment finds a deep parallel with the Joint Declaration's accomplishment as well. When asked early in his career whether he wrote as a Protestant or a Catholic, he responded:

I simply do not know. I do not believe that theology when rightly done is either Catholic or Protestant. The object of the theologian's inquiry is quite simply God—not Catholicism or Protestantism. The proper object of the qualifier "catholic" is the church, not theology or theologians. No theologian should desire anything less than that his or her theology reflect the catholic character of the church. Thus I hope my theology is catholic inasmuch as it is true to those Protestants and Roman Catholics who constitute the church catholic.[12]

11. *Joint Declaration on the Doctrine of Justification* 3.15, available at http://www.vatican.va/roman_curia/pontifical_councils/chrstuni/documents/rc_pc_chrstuni_doc_31101999_cath-luth-joint-declaration_en.html.
12. Stanley Hauerwas, *The Peaceable Kingdom: A Primer in Christian Ethics* (Notre Dame: University of Notre Dame Press, 1983), xxvi.

To turn "Catholic" or "Protestant" into identity markers for individual theologians is problematic in Hauerwas's view. As Lindbeck provided the method for reaching doctrinal convergence, Hauerwas stands within a twentieth-century christological *ressourcement* for Christian thought and life that the declaration presupposes. The simultaneous christological emphases of Karl Barth and the *nouvelle théologie* shifted the horizons of Reformation/Counter-Reformation polemic concerning justification from an "anthropological" to a "christological" center[13]—a common return to the Chalcedonian christological formula, seen, perhaps most dramatically, as the very point of convergence that links the thought of Karl Barth to *nouvelle théologie*.[14] When Protestant New Testament scholars recovered the ancient Christian teaching of justification through the faith *of*, rather than *in*, Jesus Christ,[15] theological space opened to engage the anthropological differences between the Reformation and Roman Catholic teachings.

Hauerwas, following Barth, was already there.[16] In *The Peaceable Kingdom*, his most systematic work outside his Gifford Lectures, Hauerwas had written, "The essential Christian witness is neither to personal experience, nor to what Christianity means to 'me,' but to the truth that this world is the creation of a good God who is known through the people of Israel and the life, death, and resurrection of Jesus Christ."[17] Jesus Christ is the center of

13. For this distinction between "anthropological" and "christological" understandings of the Pauline doctrine of justification, including Hauerwas's participation in this shift, see Douglas Harink, *Paul among the Postliberals: Pauline Theology beyond Christendom and Modernity* (Grand Rapids: Brazos, 2003), 25–65.

14. See Kenneth Oakes, "The Question of Nature and Grace in Karl Barth: Humanity as Creature and as Covenant-Partner," *Modern Theology* 23 (2007): 595–616.

15. See the significant work by Richard B. Hays, *The Faith of Jesus Christ: An Investigation into the Narrative Substructure of Galatians 3:1–4:11*, 2nd ed. (Grand Rapids: Eerdmans, 2001).

16. "It is precisely at this point that Hauerwas discerns the significance of Karl Barth. For Barth once again recovered Christian theology/ethics as a matter of developing a 'moral ontology' (Webster's term) in which the gospel of Jesus Christ is the all-encompassing and determinative reality and the church is the necessary context for discerning the shape of the Christian life" (Harink, *Paul among the Postliberals*, 64).

17. Hauerwas, *Peaceable Kingdom*, 15.

Hauerwas's thought, the Joint Declaration, and the hope for the visible unity of the church. As John Paul II wrote in *Ut Unum Sint*,

> "Ecumenical" prayer, as the prayer of brothers and sisters, expresses all this. Precisely because they are separated from one another, they *meet in Christ* with all the more hope, *entrusting to him the future of their unity and their communion.* Here too we can appropriately apply the teaching of the Council: "The Lord Jesus, when he prayed to the Father '*that they may be one . . . as we are one*' (John 17:21–22), opened up vistas closed to human reason. For he implied a certain likeness between the union of the Divine Persons, and the union of God's children in truth and charity."[18]

Justification takes place in the unity of believers in Jesus Christ. The church's witness of living in the peace of justification represents the very core of Hauerwas's experiment in differentiated unity with Lindbeck's. The experiment does not close in, but incorporates and unifies the church in Christ, through the Spirit, for the sake of the peace of the world.

David Burrell's experiment seems far from the Joint Declaration on Justification. His work has focused on an analytic retrieval of the doctrine of creation that Thomas worked out in dialogue with the Islamic theologian Ibn-Sina and the Jewish theologian Maimonides. Even here, though, Burrell's work on the doctrine of creation connects to the doctrine of justification within the web of Christian teaching. William Cavanaugh has connected Aquinas's doctrine of justification-as-participation with his doctrine of creation.[19] Aquinas's doctrine of creation requires that creation participate in God for its very being in a manner that eludes human language, yet is nonetheless real. While all creation participates in God for its very being, human beings may participate by sharing through Christ in

18. John Paul II, *Ut Unum Sint: On Commitment to Ecumenism*, 1995, par. 26, available at http://www.vatican.va/holy_father/john_paul_ii/encyclicals/documents/hf_jp-ii_enc_25051995_ut-unum-sint_en.html.

19. William T. Cavanaugh, "A Joint Declaration? Justification as Theosis in Luther and Aquinas," *Heythrop Journal* 41 (2000): 265–80.

the divine communion that is the Triune God. Precisely at this point, Cavanaugh points to a vein of research in Finnish Luther scholarship that suggests that Luther shared this concern with Aquinas: "Luther and Aquinas then meet at this most crucial of theological intersections between the absolute otherness of God and the divinization of the human. The being of God can fill us entirely precisely because of our emptiness—precisely because we are not God."[20]

As Cavanaugh points out, this opens up the possibility of deeper agreement within the Lutheran/Roman Catholic dialogues—which would also open up a common discourse with Eastern Orthodoxy.[21] Burrell's experiment has shown how Christian theology creatively interacted with Muslim and Jewish sources in the work of Thomas Aquinas; his work, appropriated by others, has reached out beyond the confines of "identity" theology to work for the visible reunification of the church and even a recovery of such concepts in the Pauline witness itself.[22]

The relationship between the experiments of Lindbeck, Hauerwas, and Burrell and the Joint Declaration on Justification suggests that their work has contributed directly and indirectly toward the visible unity of the church catholic—the body of Christ in the world—for the sake of the world. Their work fights against localizing and sectarian identity interests that have become standard in an expressivist culture of North America. Concerns for "identity" over the "truthfulness" of Christian claims have reduced the church to a consumerist option for causes defined by its demographic.[23] As a result, "secular

20. Ibid., 277–78.

21. See Anne N. Williams, *The Ground of Union: Deification in Aquinas and Palamas* (New York: Oxford University Press, 1999). This is the published version of Williams's Yale dissertation written under Professor Lindbeck.

22. For an argument of theosis, or participation in God through Christ, as the key for the Pauline understanding of justification, see Michael J. Gorman, *Inhabiting the Cruciform God: Kenosis, Justification, and Theosis in Paul's Narrative Soteriology* (Grand Rapids: Eerdmans, 2009).

23. *In One Body through the Cross* reads,

This tendency to transform binding norms into consumer options is not simply the result of sociological forces. It reflects a deeper spiritual malaise, which developed especially in the wake of the splintering of Western Christianity in

principles and expertise supersede Christian principles of dis-
cernment as the basis for cooperation."[24] The first-generation
postliberals have worked for the visibility and integrity of the
church's witness in the world.

The Judgment of a Public: The Communion of Saints

Trials require a jury to make a final judgment. DeHart speaks
abstractly of "a public of some sort" to judge theological proposals. He seems concerned that a "postliberal" experiment
diminishes the impact of the church's witness in the world,
what he calls the church's "effectiveness."[25] DeHart writes,
"Precisely because of its [the church's] mission, its 'sending
out,' . . . it must allow the semantic permeation of its borders
in the full critical engagement of the social and cultural logic
of its site."[26] What "public site" could most transcend narrow
cultural borders constructed by time, place, gender, and eth-
nicity to judge Lindbeck's, Burrell's, and Hauerwas's related
theological experiments?

I would like to suggest that one particular group is best qualified to judge the "postliberal" experiment. DeHart writes, "To
bear witness *to* this norm [Jesus Christ] as the liberating word
in a potential infinity of social, cultural, historical situations
properly brings witness under a complex of different kinds of
pressures from the varied 'sites' of its occurrence. Witness is

---

the sixteenth century. In every separated community the temptation has been
to base the community's life on its 'distinctives,' that is, on the features of
its faith and life that differentiate it from other Christian communities. The
apostolic faith confessed in the ecumenical creeds, intended to differentiate
the church from truly spurious 'Christian' communities, is pushed to the
margin of communal self-description. (Jenson and Braaten, *In One Body
through the Cross*, 39)

24. Ibid., 47.

25. DeHart writes, "Witness (and hence theology) demands a missiological submission to the judgment of the world as to the effectiveness of its word" (*Trial of
the Witnesses*, 268).

26. Ibid., 245.

'normed' by Jesus Christ alone, but it is 'tried' at its site."[27] The group most qualified to judge the appeal of the "postliberals" is the communion of saints.

The loss of awareness of the communion of saints has diminished recent discourses on the church by professional theologians. Earlier in this book we discussed the cultural transformations of the 1960s and the expressivist presuppositions that accompanied them. We can attribute the loss of awareness of the communion of saints to the "immanent frame"—the limiting of theological discourse to an underlying historicism—that has emerged from these changes. Read within a narrow historicist framework, the postliberal understanding of the church seems locked within a very limited ecclesial repetition to sustain an ingrown "identity."

The appeal of the postliberals exceeds such limits in its *ressourcement*, a *ressourcement* that seeks to honor the witness of the saints who prepare the way for God in Christ by the Spirit to raise up new generations. Seen within the context of the communion of saints, the church catholic is very different from the church global; its catholicity transcends time as well as space even as its catholicity is always found within particular cultural spaces and a very specific historical time. The saints point human life toward the transcendence of their participation in Christ in the historically determined but common witness to the sanctifying work of the Holy Spirit.

The communion of saints allows us to appeal to the commonality-in-historical-and-cultural-difference of Theresa of Calcutta and Dorothy Day and Edith Stein and Clare of Assisi and Macrina the Younger and Perpetua—and countless others like them whom God has raised up in geographic and temporal localities within the church catholic, those like Lillian Smith and Alice Brown.[28] The communion of saints shows that

27. Ibid., 249–50.

28. Alice Brown and Lillian Smith were elderly parishioners of mine in the Winamac Church of the Nazarene, whose holiness was a model for all those who encountered them. When they both moved into the county nursing home, it was the hospital staff, supposedly there to care for their bodily needs, who regularly would gather in their rooms for joint prayer and wisdom and support from Lillian and Alice. Alice, with

the church's witness does not arise merely from a "semantic permeation" of a particular social and cultural site's borders and logic; the communion of saints shows that there are no borders for the embodied witness to the gospel to permeate. The embodied critical engagement that a holy witness provides within a particular social and cultural site reveals how such sites are not annulled, but are raised and purified in Christ.

The communion of saints, confessed in the Apostles' Creed, has surprisingly emerged as a point of convergence in recent work toward the visible unity of the church catholic.[29] All Christians affirm that "the communion of saints is the communion of justified sinners."[30] From this basis in the justification provided by the Triune God, the language of the "communion of the saints" works simultaneously at different levels. The communion of the saints incorporates all the "justified sinners" even as it holds up for emulation those whose lives provide exemplary, embodied models of holiness:

> The saints comprise "a great multitude that no one can count, from every nation, from all peoples and languages" (Rev. 7:9). At the same time, some persons from this multitude have left their mark on the memory of the church in special ways, persons who have lived and died as exemplary disciples of Christ in the community of faith of their time. To this group belong, first of all, those who have spilled their blood in witness to the faith (*martyrs*) and also later ascetics and confessors. Saints in

---

missionary friends around the world for whom she prayed daily, was more informed about the affairs of the world than anyone I knew; when I, trained in the modern therapeutic psychological pastoral "wisdom," asked Lillian if she was angry about having to move from her farm to the nursing home, she looked at me and expressed, without pride, "Angry? I don't get angry anymore." I believed her.

29. See, for instance, "The Communion of Saints: A Statement of Evangelicals and Catholics Together," *First Things*, March 2003, available at http://www.firstthings.com/article/2007/01/the-communion-of-saints-17; Bilateral Working Group of the German National Bishops' Conference and the Church Leadership of the United Evangelical Lutheran Church of Germany, *Communio Sanctorum: The Church as the Communion of Saints*, trans. Mark W. Jeske, Michael Root, and Daniel R. Smith (Collegeville, MN: Liturgical Press, 2004); and the centrality of the concept in John Paul II's encyclical *Ut Unum Sint*.

30. Bilateral Working Group, *Communio Sanctorum*, 33, par. 90.

this sense are those members of the church who solely by grace
and faith have lived out love and other Christian virtues in an
exemplary fashion and whose witness has found recognition
in the church after their death. They all comprise the "cloud of
witnesses" (Heb. 12:1) with whom the communion of saints on
earth has a permanent union.[31]

The communion of saints requires a paradoxical logic of both/
and. The communion of saints is simultaneously local and catholic, past and present and future, and comprised of justified sinners
and holy exemplars. The communion of saints is also simultaneously invisible and visible. As Francesca Murphy notes, "The
Communion of the Saints is, in one way, as 'invisible' as the eschatological, immaculate church, but, in another way, the Saints are
familiar fixtures: we have palpable evidence that these personages
have emerged, by God's will, in every Christian setting."[32]

The ability of the Holy Spirit to form saints as bodily exemplars of holiness in all ecclesial communions provides hope
for the work toward the visible unity of the church catholic.
Such concrete, embodied witnesses provide the backdrop for
the postliberals' work and thought. In his encyclical *Ut Unum
Sint*, John Paul II recognized the particular significance of the
martyrs for ecumenical work: "Despite the tragedy of our divisions, these brothers and sisters have preserved an attachment to
Christ and to the Father so radical and absolute as to lead even
to the shedding of blood."[33] The "communion of the martyrs

31. Ibid., 77, par. 229.
32. Francesca Aran Murphy, "De Lubac, Ratzinger, and von Balthasar: A Communal Adventure in Ecclesiology," in *Ecumenism Today: The Universal Church in
the 21st Century*, ed. Francesca Aran Murphy and Christopher Asprey (Burlington,
VT: Ashgate, 2008), 75.
33. John Paul II, *Ut Unum Sint*, par. 83. John Paul similarly writes,
   In a theocentric vision, we Christians already have a common Martyrology.
   This also includes the martyrs of our own century, more numerous than one
   might think, and it shows how, at a profound level, God preserves communion among the baptized in the supreme demand of faith, manifested in the
   sacrifice of life itself. . . . This communion is already perfect in what we all
   consider the highest point of the life of grace, martyria unto death, the truest
   communion possible with Christ who shed his Blood, and by that sacrifice
   brings near those who once were far off (cf. Eph 2:13). (par. 84)

and the saints" goads the church, often against herself, toward a visible unity in light of the unity God has already accomplished in the communion of the saints. As John Paul II writes, "In the radiance of the 'heritage of the saints' belonging to all Communities, the 'dialogue of conversion' towards full and visible unity thus appears as a source of hope. This universal presence of the Saints is in fact a proof of the transcendent power of the Spirit. It is the sign and proof of God's victory over the forces of evil which divide humanity."[34]

The saints do not allow the church's witness to collapse inward to an enclosed "identity" within the Christian tradition. Francesca Murphy again summarizes, "By transgressing 'Christian' boundaries, the saints show us the invisible church within the visible morass of mutually hostile 'communions.' Their God-given holiness is evidence for the faith that 'it is not our, but his, Church.'"[35] The jury of the communion of saints, particularly those exemplary among them, will not countenance any sectarian collapse inward for the purity of the church's identity contrasted against its mission.

How would those exemplars within this visible/invisible jury of the communion of saints judge the postliberals? How would this "public" that has negotiated the boundaries between the church and the world in witness view the work of Lindbeck, Burrell, and Hauerwas? While one cannot speak definitively until the end of all things, one cannot help but think that they would approve. Lindbeck's experiment refuses an easy harmonization or solution to previous disagreements within the church catholic. To do so would exclude the holy witnesses of those within the specific traditions of the church, those whose witness has come before us from the communion of saints in the integrity of their witness. By looking at how shifting backgrounds can reconfigure the language used to allow a convergence—a common agreement behind the different languages—Lindbeck's experiment also renders intelligible how there is a single communion of

34. Ibid.
35. Murphy, "De Lubac, Ratzinger, and von Balthasar," 75.

saints, that visible/invisible cloud of witnesses drawn from all communions into eternal communion in Christ.

Lindbeck's whole experiment protects the unity of the communion of saints from present expressivist endeavors to diminish the exemplary witnesses, known and unknown, of the past. The present church cannot exclude past witnesses, even as they recognize that they too were/are justified sinners. Lindbeck's experiment not only seeks to work for a visible unity for the future life of the church; he also refuses to exclude the invisible unity of the communion of the saints from the past, those who have successfully lived across those permeable boundaries between the church and the world.

Hauerwas similarly draws upon the visible witness of the invisible communion of saints to show how the witness of the church corresponds with the grain of the universe. Hauerwas often invokes various saints, present and historical, as an ethical resource to guide the imagination of the church in its witness to the world today. What is more subtle, however, in Hauerwas's work is how he presupposes and embraces the communion of saints through such allusions. For instance, in an essay in his recent *The State of the University*, Hauerwas subtly appeals to an essay by the radical Reformation theologian John Howard Yoder that refers to the significance of the saints and bishops to ensure the visible witness of the church: "Yoder's calling attention to the significance of the lives of the saints, and the office of the bishop necessary to sustain such lives, is but a reminder that a world was and can be sustained by the sacrament of reconciliation."[36] Only the communion of the saints dispels the irony of a radical Reformation theologian invoking the saints, the office of the bishop, and the sacrament of reconciliation. Hauerwas mentions the common witness among the saints of different ecclesial communities because of his conviction that the shared visible holiness of the communion of saints transcends the historical and cultural particularities in which God formed

36. Stanley Hauerwas, "The Gospel and Cultural Formations," in *The State of the University: Academic Knowledge and the Knowledge of God* (Oxford: Blackwell, 2007), 41.

their witness. The contemporary church catholic's participation in the visible/invisible communion of saints shows "the
necessity of witness."[37] Hauerwas's project seeks to make the
peaceableness of the invisible communion of saints normative
for the visible communion in the world today. It would seem
that such an experiment would likewise receive the applause of
the saints for the sake of the glory and praise of God.

What of David Burrell's work? Again, Burrell has asked
ontological questions and interfaced with various traditions
outside the faith given to the saints in their own confessions
about God. One should not miss, however, that his return to
Thomas as a model for interfaith dialogue presupposes a historic communion of saints. Whereas the modernist caricature
of medieval theology is one of intolerance and irrationality
and exclusivity, Burrell's academic analysis of the medieval interaction of Maimonides, Ibn-Sina, and Aquinas shows the
ongoing importance of contemporary theological discourse
with the other Abrahamic faiths (something in which Burrell
himself has participated).[38] For Burrell, Thomas does not stand
above criticism—after all, Aquinas was a justified sinner. Yet

37. The phrase is the title of chapter 8 of Hauerwas's Gifford lectures, *With the
Grain of the Universe: The Church's Witness and Natural Theology* (Grand Rapids:
Brazos, 2001), 205–41. In this chapter Hauerwas discusses the similarities between
John Howard Yoder's and John Paul II's witness:

> Of course there are many witnesses I could have chosen other than John
> Howard Yoder and John Paul II. Theologians and popes are seldom counted
> among the most determinative witnesses to the gospel—a point, no doubt,
> that Yoder and the pope would be the first to make. I am sure that they would
> both argue that the countless nameless Christians that have lived lives faithful
> to the gospel are more likely subjects than either of them for witnessing the
> faith. I have no reason to doubt that they would be right to direct attention to
> others. But John Howard Yoder and John Paul II are theologically articulate
> witnesses whose witness has required them to say why the truth of what the
> church proclaims cannot be known as truth without witnesses; thus given
> what I have tried to articulate in these lectures, they are particularly good
> witnesses. (217–18)

Given the ecclesial, social, and historical differences between John Howard Yoder
and John Paul II, only a deep conviction in the communion of saints renders such a
statement intelligible.

38. See Stanley Hauerwas, "The End of 'Religious Pluralism': A Tribute to David
Burrell, CSC," in *State of the University*, 58–75.

Thomas's intellectual interaction with the Jewish and Islamic communities bears a sign of transcendence for contemporary emulation. Burrell stands within the communion of saints and pursues his work in honor of those who worthily came before. He thus continues a long tradition in the church with figures such as John of Damascus and Thomas Aquinas whose articulation of the Christian faith has taken place within the very context of interaction with Jews and Muslims.

Such is the appeal of the witnesses. If a lawyer imposed an artificial narrative to try to persuade a jury of the defendant's guilt, perhaps that jury would find these witnesses guilty of diminishing the type of Christian mission presupposed by that abstracted narrative. Heard, however, within a narrative of their experiments within, for, and toward the visible church catholic, their witness rings faithful and true. Semantic permutations are never a substitute for the substantial bodily presence of the church; the first-generation postliberals recognize that theological language serves bodily practice, not as something different, but as a necessary component of the church catholic itself. In this, paradoxically, they both depend upon and join the communion of saints, local and catholic; visible and invisible; past, present, and future; justified sinners and holy exemplars.

Is Protestantism Over?

The first-generation postliberals have sought to continue, even as they have presupposed, the post–World War movement toward the visible unification of the church. They have engaged the witness and mission of the church in its current fragmentation even as they have sought to retrieve its witness in happier times when the visible unity of the church was apparent. If the Joint Declaration on the Doctrine of Justification symbolizes in some ways their victory, the muted reception of the Joint Declaration in the churches throughout the world highlights their defeat.[39]

39. While the document has also received formal approval by ecclesial bodies such as the World Methodist Council, the agreement has made little, if any, impact on the

In the initial wake of the Joint Declaration, at least two books published in North America pressed the question, "Is the Reformation over?"[40] Of course, it is obvious that it is not; we have seen that the church in the West is in the process of new fragmentations, new reconfigurations, new modes of cultural accommodation and renewal. The forces that unleashed the Reformation and its doppelgänger, the Counter-Reformation, still wreak their havoc on the church catholic.

It is characteristic of the work of Stanley Hauerwas to reframe the question. Hauerwas wonders "whether we may be coming to a time when the story we call the 'Reformation' will not determine our understanding of where we are as Protestant Christians." He continues:

> We may be living during a time when we are watching Protestantism coming to an end. What that means for the future I am not sure. The very name "Protestant" denotes a protest movement, a reform movement, in the church catholic. When Protestantism became an end in itself, when Protestants become denominations, we became unintelligible to ourselves. Our inability to resist the market, our inability as Protestants not to become consumers of our religious preferences, is but an indication that we are in trouble. Of course, Roman Catholicism is also beset

---

local churches themselves. Benedict XVI indicated this in his visit to Regensburg, Germany, in 2006. According to John Radano:

> Referring to [Benedict XVI's] many memories his visit there evoked, [Benedict stated], "Obviously I think in particular of the demanding efforts to reach a consensus on justification. I recall all the stages of that process of the memorable meeting with the late Bishop Hanselmann here in Regensburg—a meeting that contributed decisively to the achievement of the conclusion." He then made an important pastoral observation. "The agreement on justification," he said, "remains an important task which—in my view—is not yet fully accomplished," because "in theology, justification is an essential theme, but in the life of the faithful today—it seems to me—it is only dimly present." He continued illustrating the need for a rediscovery of God in our midst. (See *Lutheran and Catholic Reconciliation on Justification*, 204–5)

40. See Mark Noll and Carolyn Nystrom, *Is the Reformation Over? An Evangelical Assessment of Contemporary Roman Catholicism* (Grand Rapids: Baker Academic, 2005); and Geoffrey Wainwright, *Is the Reformation Over? Catholics and Protestants at the Turn of the Millennium* (Milwaukee: Marquette University Press, 2000).

by the challenge of choice, which helps explain why Catholicism in America may now be a form of Protestantism.[41]

The institutional weakening of mainline Protestantism (and the "protestantizing" of American Roman Catholic churches), the way that evangelicals speak of "natural congregational cycles of rise and decline," the overtaking of Protestant congregations by the American political right or left, all suggest that Hauerwas's statements are not the statements of a provocateur. His observation recognizes that a church determined by choice, by human will, remains unstable and unable to sustain its witness over time. The history of the Protestant church in the United States records precisely such instability.[42] Perhaps the first-generation postliberals' greatest gift to the church in North America is their refusal to reduce the church to a free association of believers determined by human will.

Mark Noll summarizes the underlying difference between American Protestant evangelical and Roman Catholic understanding of the church in terms of the priority of the individual's choice: "For Catholics, the church constitutes believers; for evangelicals believers constitute the church. For Catholics, individual believers are a function of the church; for evangelicals, the church is a function of individual believers."[43] With the assertion of the priority of the individual believer, it is no wonder that the church in the United States cannot resist the temptation "to become consumers of our religious preferences."

The bifurcation in which Noll frames the ecclesiological issue, however, brings to mind a concern that Congar expressed in *Divided Christendom* about the potentiality of reunion with

41. Stanley Hauerwas, "The End of Protestantism and the Methodist Contribution," *Wesleyan Theological Journal* 41 (2006), 8.

42. See Roger Finke and Rodney Stark, *The Churching of America 1776–1990* (Piscataway, NJ: Rutgers University Press, 1990); see also "Eclipsing the Biblical Narrative: The Narrative Contours of North American Christianity," in John W. Wright, *Telling God's Story: Narrative Preaching for Christian Formation* (Downers Grove, IL: IVP Academic, 2007), 47–76.

43. Noll and Nystrom, *Is the Reformation Over?* 238.

Protestants. Congar saw a fundamental instability in Protestant tendencies:

> Protestantism presents two outstanding features—particular objects of belief and a particular way of approaching and interpreting religious reality. We believe that the latter of these is always inimical to the former; that the specifically Protestant mind is gradually destructive of the objects of its own belief, and of what survives of the heritage of historic Christianity. This habit of mind consists in continually setting in opposition things which ought to be held together, properly articulated, and harmonized.[44]

What Congar did not see, and what recent scholarship has recently made more evident, is the underlying emphasis on the divine will and divine voluntarism (ironically, inherited from medieval Catholicism) that had become embedded, to various degrees, in Protestantism, particularly within modernity.[45] Protestants see the church as constituted by believers in contrast to believers being constituted by the church; for instance, Henri de Lubac in his work *Catholicism* would never frame the issue as the priority of church or individual believer. Within the very catholicity of the church, participation in God through Christ by the Holy Spirit constitutes the church catholic. Locating the church's origin in the Triune God, de Lubac substitutes the paradox of a both/and of Christian community and individual believer for a Protestant (and modernist Roman Catholic) either/or of priority of Christian community or individual believer.[46]

44. Congar, *Divided Christendom*, 273–74.

45. See David Burrell, "Review of Michael Allen Gillespie, *The Theological Origins of Modernity*," *Notre Dame Philosophical Reviews*, November 9, 2008, available at http://ndpr.nd.edu/review.cfm?id=14665.

46. For example, de Lubac writes, "In the man in whom the grace of Christ triumphs over sin it will be seen that the most spiritual inwardness is coincident with the fullness of the Catholic spirit, a spirit, that is to say, of the broadest universality coupled with the strictest unity. . . . For the fact that he 'has received the Spirit of God and that the Spirit of God dwells in him' may be recognized precisely in this: 'the love of peace and unity, the love of the Church scattered far and wide over the face of the earth'" (Henri de Lubac, *Catholicism: Christ and the Common Destiny of Man* [San Francisco:

An understanding of the church catholic that prioritizes either community or individual merely repeats the logic of modern liberal politics with its roots in an opposition between the general and the individual will. Attempting to solve the instability through dialectic does not help. Anchored in the human will, whether individual or communal, the catholicity of the church will be lost, its witness diminished, and eventually it will be reabsorbed back into the liberal society that has been more determinative for it than the gospel.

In 1929 a young German Lutheran theologian recognized that a church anchored in human will cannot sustain its witness over time. His work found no publisher for several years; fortunately he came from a wealthy background and was able to subsidize the costs for its publication. In this first book, his doctoral dissertation, he wrote,

> If the church consummated in Christ is to build itself up in time, the will of God must constantly be realized anew, no longer acting as a general principle for all men, but in the personal appropriation of individual men; and this appropriation is possible only upon the ground of God's action in Christ, and presupposes both the being of mankind in the church (which is consummated in Christ) and the bringing of the individual into the church, that is, into the humanity of Christ, by the act of appropriation.[47]

Though Protestant—and because of his immersion in the Christian Scriptures—he rejected an understanding of the church grounded in the will of believers: "Communion with God exists

---

Ignatius, 1988], 79–80). Likewise, see his discussion on the sacraments in the same work: "Since the sacraments are the means of salvation they should be understood as instruments of unity. As they make real, renew or strengthen man's union with Christ, by that very fact they make real, renew or strengthen his union with the Christian community" (82). For the significance of paradox as characteristic of de Lubac's thought, and its relationship with Kierkegaard, see Eric Lee, "From Copenhagen to Cambrai: Paradoxes of Faith in Kierkegaard and de Lubac," in *Belief and Metaphysics*, ed. Peter M. Candler Jr. and Conor Cunningham (London: SCM, 2007), 236–59.

47. Dietrich Bonhoeffer, *The Communion of Saints: A Dogmatic Inquiry into the Sociology of the Church*, trans. Ronald Smith (New York: Harper & Row, 1960), 104.

only through Christ, but Christ is present only in his church, hence there is communion with God only in the church. . . . The church does not come into being through people coming together (genetic sociology). But it is in being through the Spirit which is effective in the community. So it cannot be derived from individual wills. . . . In the Word which comes to the individual both the perfected communion of saints and the communion of saints developing itself in time are equally present."[48]

Dietrich Bonhoeffer, the author of these words, worked for the moral and political integrity of the witness of the church catholic as he worked for its visible unity. One can find an ecclesial overlap between his *Sanctorum Communio* and de Lubac's *Catholicism*, an overlap that empowered the renewal of the church, Protestant and Catholic, after the atrocities of World War II. Their work joined in a thrust toward a unity in the visible communion of saints that would more fully participate in the unity of the invisible, eschatological communion of saints. Protestants in North America had their historic emphasis on the church as constructed through individual believers accentuated by a modernism (and postmodernism) that it helped create; it is no surprise that such an ecclesiology, anchored in the human will, could not sustain this vision through the cultural and institutional changes of the 1960s.

George Lindbeck, David Burrell, and Stanley Hauerwas stand with Bonhoeffer at the end of Protestantism. In many ways they themselves have protested Protestantism and how "the specifically Protestant mind is gradually destructive of the objects of its own belief." This does not mean that the Reformation is over. Their lives, writings, conversations, and friendship witness (across the division of their own ecclesial traditions) to the communion of saints; this makes it ever more tragic that they have never experienced a common life together in Christ at the Eucharistic feast. Mourning this tragedy and in honor of their exemplary witness, we must carry on their cause for the integrity of the witness of a visibly unified church catholic.

48. Ibid., 116.

Index

157